the complete guide to the

puppy

the complete guide to the
puppy

sarah whitehead

THALAMUS
PUBLISHING

Complete Guide to the Puppy

Text and design © 2000 Thalamus Publishing

Thalamus Publishing

an imprint of

International Media Solutions Limited

4 Attorney's Walk, Bull Ring, Ludlow, Shropshire SY8 1AA, England

Commissioning editor: Lucian Randall

Project editor: Warren Lapworth

Jacket design: Thalamus Studios

Interior design: Paul Chubb

Repro: Prima Media Ltd

ISBN 1-902886-01-1

Printed and bound in India by Thomson Press

Picture Acknowledgments

Picture research by Image Select International Limited

Animals Unlimited: 121; Marc Henrie, Asc: 134 top, 142, 143; Image Bank: (Elyse Lewin) 82; RSPCA Photolibrary: (JB Blossom) 35 top, 117, (Des Cartwright) 127, (Cheryl A Ertelt) 90, 125 top, (Andrew Forsyth) 87 top, 87 left, 87 bottom, 88, (Mark Hamblin) 67 top, (Angela Hampton) 7 top, 33, 45, 47 top, 56, 57, 61, 62, 65, 67 bottom, 73, 76, 96, 99, 101, (EA Janes) 9, 68, (Andrew Linscott) 72, (Ken McKay) 38-39, 103, 123, 129, (Colin Seddon) 70, 78; Spectrum Colour Library: 2–3, 7 bottom, 50, 54, 69 top, 71, 74-75, 75, 89, 104, 107, 116, (G.Carlisle) 106; SuperStock: 93, 130, 131; Warren Photographic: (Jane Burton) 1, 6, 8, 10, 11, 12, 13, 14, 15, 16, 17, 18, 19, 20, 21, 22, 23, 24, 25, 26, 27, 28, 29, 30, 31, 32, 34, 35 bottom, 36, 37, 39, 40, 41, 42, 43, 44, 46, 47 bottom, 48, 49, 51, 52, 53, 55, 58, 59, 60, 63, 64, 66, 69 bottom, 77, 79, 80, 81 top, 81 bottom, 83, 84, 85, 86, 91, 92, 94, 95, 97, 98, 100, 102, 105, 108, 109, 110, 111, 112, 113, 114, 115, 118, 119, 120, 122 bottom, 124, 125 bottom, 126, 128, 133, 134 bottom, 136, 137 top, 137 bottom, 138, 139 top, 139 bottom, 140, 141, (Kim Taylor) 122 top, 132, 135.

table of

contents

introduction

Buying a puppy is one of the most exciting and rewarding experiences in life. Full of expectations for the future and armed with lots of practical information, owners can quickly and easily settle the newcomer into their homes and enjoy the next weeks and months of their new dog's

left *Six years old and six weeks old—the beginning of a lifelong friendship.*

development as it unfolds before them. Puppies are cute, fun, loving, and intelligent. They can also be frustrating, mischievous and the greatest time-wasters on Earth!

To ensure that your puppy grows up to be confident and happy, it is vital to realize that your new pet is not a small person in disguise but a fully functioning animal, ready equipped with instincts, drives, and even weaponry to carry out all the actions of a predator. Dogs bark, chew, freely urinate, dig, run, jump, chase, and bite, all as a part of their normal repertoire. They behave in ways most humans find hard to understand—or even totally unacceptable—and they have no moral values to judge or be judged by! Normal puppy behavior is often misinterpreted by owners, who need to realize that each and every puppy needs to learn how to become not only a dog, but more importantly, a pet dog.

Every puppy is born with a blueprint for life. Many of his or her characteristics, as well as the way that the puppy looks, is predetermined by breed, parental influences, and even what happened to the puppy while in the womb. However, the second that the puppy enters the world, influences on the development of this blueprint begin. This is

where our efforts make a difference—a puppy's upbringing can make or break that adult dog's behavior and character.

In order to fulfil his or her potential, each puppy needs to be fully domesticated. This means teaching them what is appropriate behavior and what isn't, and how to interact with children, dogs, and other animals. It also means learning how to behave in the home and how to act when taken out for walks in both town and countryside. All dogs need socialization and training that follow a deliberate structure if they are to become valued members of our society.

The first weeks and months of owning a puppy offer a chance to shape your pet's behavior and character for the rest of his or her life. This period is fun and exciting, but is over incredibly quickly. Whatever the breed or type of your puppy, enjoy these early days and make the most of them. Welcome to the world of dogs!

above *A young dog soon becomes part of the family—for life.*

below *All breeds of puppy enjoy toys and companionship.*

when does a puppy become a dog?

what is a dog?

Dogs fulfil many roles in modern society. They can be companions and workers—performing a job such a police dog or guide dog for the blind. They can be trained as helpers for the disabled and perform complex tasks such as loading a washing machine or switching lights on and off. Other dogs have even been trained to warn their owners that they are going to have an epileptic seizure, giving the person time to reach a safe place before the onset of an attack. Dogs of all kinds in many countries search for lost people in mountainous regions and after urban and environmental disasters.

However, by far the most important roles for millions of dogs is that of a good pet. The dog has been man's companion for thousands of years—hunting with him, guarding his property, and providing companionship and loyalty. In a fast-changing world, friendship with another creature is more important than ever and this is where dogs blossom and flourish—forming strong, lifelong bonds with their human owners.

Despite this deep attachment to man, dogs are still dogs. We must never forget that dogs are predators descended from the wolf, animals designed to hunt and kill for survival. Their teeth alone are a testimony to this legacy. Large canine teeth and impressive speed remain in nearly all present-day breeds, while other features, such as ear shape and length of coat, have been altered beyond recognition. Dogs retain many of their ancestor's characteristics, and the vast majority will still attempt to stalk, chase, bite, and "kill"—even if only in play!

Puppies are born with a set of characteristics that equip them for a life in the wild, not a place in our homes. It is a wonderful measure of their adaptability that with socialization, training, love, and care, dogs come to live as a part of our families and give so much in return. Dogs offer humans the best of both worlds—the chance to see a real animal in action, with all its instincts, drives, and wild behavior, and the opportunity to build a relationship with a domesticated creature.

reaching maturity

Puppies do not stay puppies for long! Their growth rate and developmental progress are incredibly fast, particularly when compared with that of humans. As soon as puppies lose their deciduous teeth at around 18 to 20 weeks old, they can no longer be considered true puppies.

However, after this time, dogs still have much growing and maturing to do. Many breeds, particularly the larger ones, do not fully mature physically until they are at least three years old—and their mental development may take even longer! Indeed, while most dogs become calmer and more considered in their behavior after the age of three or four, some individuals never seem to grow up. Perhaps this is their very fascination—for in enjoying our dogs' puppyish behavior, we retain some of our child-like qualities, too!

right *As they mature dogs can become workers, such as Border Collies that help farmers to herd sheep.*

age equivalence
and development rates

Puppies grow at an incredible rate. Their minds and bodies develop much more rapidly than humans do, so at the age of only two years a dog may be physically and mentally mature. Sadly, this developmental rate not only means that puppyhood is over in a flash, it also means that compared to humans, dogs have a short life span, too.

How quickly a puppy matures and how long he or she will eventually live is partly determined by genes and partly by lifestyle. Just like humans, fitness can be altered, depending on exercise, diet, and even stress.

Adult dog's age in human years according to weight

| Dog's age | Dog's weight | | | | |
	15.5–29lb	29–48.5lb	48.5–75lb	75–99lb	100lb+
1	12	13	15	17	20
2	19	19	21	23	26
3	25	25	27	29	32
4	30	31	32	34	37
5	35	36	37	39	42
6	40	40	42	44	47
7	44	45	46	49	52
8	48	49	51	53	57
9	52	53	55	57	62
10	55	56	59	62	67
11	59	60	63	66	72
12	62	64	67	71	77
13	66	67	71	76	83
14	69	71	76	81	90
15	73	75	80	86	96
16	77	80	85	92	104
17	82	84	91	99	112
18	86	89	97	106	121
19	91	95	103	114	131
20	97	101	111	122	142

However, one factor above all others affects a dog's longevity—and that is its size. As a rule, the larger the dog, the shorter his or her life span will be. Some of the giant breeds can be considered elderly at only eight years old, while many of

left *Equivalent ages: 18-month toddler Luke bends to pat a puppy of three weeks.*

the tiny dogs can be expected to live well into their teens. This difference between breeds means that the traditional way of comparing dog and human ages—seven dog years to one human year—is inaccurate for most breeds and types.

Puppy development compared to humans'

(Based on a medium-sized mongrel)

Dog's Age	Equivalent Human Age
2–8 weeks	1–2-year-old child
4–8 weeks	3–4-year-old child
8–12 weeks	5–7-year-old child
12–18 weeks	8–11-year-old child
5–8 months	11–14-year-old child
9–12 months	15–17-year-old child

development
of body and mind

nature versus nurture?

Just like human babies, puppies come into the world with a set of characteristics that they have inherited from their parents, as well as the incredible potential to learn and develop according to their experiences and environment. It is almost impossible to determine which has the greatest influence—nature and nurture go hand in hand and cannot be split.

right *Learning the language—yellow Labrador pups at six weeks old.*

However, while a puppy's appearance is predetermined by its mother and father, and even the genetic influence of past generations, its behavior can be affected—for good or bad—by its owners, particularly during those early weeks.

Puppies are born with basic functions. These develop over time into the skills and speed for which dogs are renown. However, puppies are not born with the skills to communicate with their own species, or human beings—they need to learn "languages" just as we do. This takes time and practice and requires input from other dogs as well as people to ensure the process is a success. Dogs kept in socially deprived environments still know how to jump and run, but cannot interact with their own kind, nor communicate with people.

learning to learn

One of the main reasons why dogs and man have had such a close and successful relationship through the centuries is because dogs are social creatures that have the ability to learn from their experiences. Dogs find out how to relate to members of their own species, in order to minimize conflict and work as a team—essential for the domestic dog's ancestors when hunting for food. They form bonds with those they live with and become attached to them—as we do to them. They discover what makes us reward them and what doesn't.

Dogs also need to learn how to learn. This may sound obvious, but research has shown that dogs that are given plenty of stimulation and opportunities for learning are more likely to solve problems in day-to-day life and find it easier to learn new skills and solve tasks.

teamwork

Rearing and caring for a puppy can be hard work, fascinating, fun, and even infuriating at times, but it is essential that sufficient time and energy is put aside to invest in this critical period of a dog's life. The first 12 weeks of your puppy's life determine his or her behavior forever. Obviously, much of this time is spent with the pup's mother, littermates, and the breeder, but there is still much that can be done to ensure a well-balanced, happy, and healthy dog for life.

above *Life is one big adventure at 10 weeks old. Pups are particularly likely to investigate smelly items!*

Understanding how your puppy has developed from birth to the present is a fascinating journey. Every period that your puppy goes through is a specialized stage that builds on the previous development but is also complete in itself. Puppies of only a few days old have reflexes that are essential to their survival but which fade and disappear as time passes and they become able to function independently.

Puppyhood passes incredibly quickly. No matter what your pup's stage of development, make sure you enjoy it!

the first week: birth and the neonatal phase

Puppies are usually born head-first. Covered in the birth membrane, they need to be licked clean by their mother before they can breathe freely. The stimulating action of the mother's tongue also helps to dry them and keep them warm.

Blind and deaf, newborn pups are entirely reliant on their mother's care, although they have a strong rooting reflex and can crawl up to 10 feet to find their mother's teats and body heat. This is a remarkable feat for a tiny puppy, which unlike many other mammals is relatively undeveloped at birth.

Throughout this stage of a puppy's development—the neonatal phase— pups detect their mother's body heat and locate her teats through a combination of heat receptors and smell receptors—all of which are located in the pup's nose. Indeed, the importance of these receptors at this time is apparent by the fact that a newborn puppy's nose seems to take up a disproportionate amount of its face!

Puppies cannot regulate their body temperature until they are between seven and ten days old, so an external heat source, such as a heat lamp, may be required. Puppies also huddle together and lie close to their mother to share body heat.

At this stage, puppies are unable to urinate or defecate by themselves. Elimination of waste products is dependent upon their mother licking them to stimulate these functions; she will usually eat the waste to keep the nest site clean as well.

right *The nose of this day-old Labrador Retriever puppy looks huge!*

The neonatal period is dominated by sleeping and eating. During this time the average litter eats for approximately 30 percent of the time and sleeps for the rest!

behavioral development
Growth and brain development begins in the neonatal period, as well as behaviors that last throughout the dog's life. Many puppies of only one day old can already make several different noises, such as whining, mewing, grunting, and even screaming. These vocalizations alert the mother if a puppy strays too far from the nest, is in pain or distress, or is being squashed by another pup or the dam (mother). At one week old, most puppies can also yelp.

above *Totally dependent on Mom, this newborn puppy is blind, deaf, and helpless.*

At this early stage it is almost impossible for the pups' mother to ignore their cries. Indeed, most mothers will leave the nest to follow a tape recording of her puppies, even if it is played some distance from her.

above *At only one day old, pups can detect warmth and scent.*

action time!

The first days after birth are sensitive ones for both puppies and mother. It is essential that the pups are kept warm, clean, and dry, and have their first contact with human beings and the world around them.

tail docking

Traditionally, several breeds of dog are docked during their first week of life. This procedure involves amputating the tail at the desired length, usually with surgical scissors. There is no doubt that this outdated procedure causes pain. The tail is an extension of the spine, and as such carries nerves and pain receptors in the same way that all limbs do. Furthermore, docking may hinder the puppies' communication system later in life and impede their balance; tails are used to express emotions and act like a rudder, in water and on land. In many countries, tail-docking by anyone other than a veterinary surgeon is illegal.

Although puppies are blind and deaf in their first two to three weeks, their sense of smell is already active and they can feel a certain amount, too, so familiarity with humans can begin right away. Puppies can be held, very gently, for short periods of time. This means that physical checks can be made and the puppy's weight monitored, while at the same time giving the puppy a chance to be handled.

The pup's brain capacity is still developing. The puppy is still too young to learn about the intricacies of the environment or communication, but the foundation stones of behavior are being laid. Indeed, it has been found that puppies who have experienced mild stress early in their lives develop a better capacity to deal with stressful situations later on. Gently picking up puppies and removing them from the proximity of their mother and handling them is a form of low-level stress and repeating this process on a frequent basis develops "stress immunization"—preparing the pups for later life.

Newborn puppies are so dependent on their mother's ability to nurture

them that they quickly lose heat and die if she is not constantly attentive. In situations where the mother is unable to feed or care for her puppies, the best alternative is always a foster mother—if one can be found. This is because rearing puppies is far more than simply feeding and cleaning them: behavioral implications start

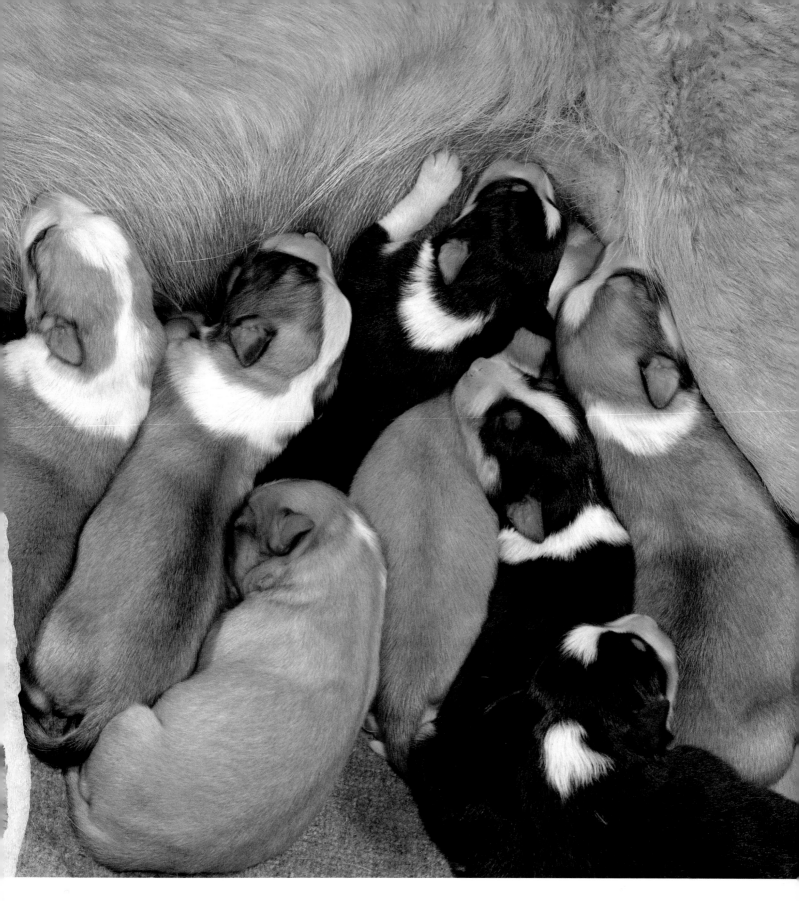

incredibly early and the best individual to teach puppies how to behave is always another dog. If a foster mother cannot be found, hand-rearing puppies is an option—but one that involves good behavioral understanding of pups' needs, as well as the commitment to feed the pups every two hours, day and night.

The majority of puppies are born with their front dew claws present and a minority have dew claws on their hind feet, too. Dew claws are the equivalent of the human thumb—made obsolete by evolution. While some veterinarians recommend the removal of either or both sets of extra digits, the vast majority of dogs live

above *Newborn pups snuggle close to share warmth, as well as suckle from their mother.*

with them perfectly happily. Provided that the claw on each toe is kept well clipped back, they rarely snag on anything.

2–4 weeks:
the transitional phase

This stage is so named because many changes take place—in terms of physical development and behavioral growth. In the third week of life, puppies are subject to incredible neurological development: their ears open and their eyes can focus on light and moving objects. While neither of these senses is fully functioning until around five weeks of age, it means that puppies can hear loud noises—and be startled by them—and see each other, their mother, and us.

physical growth

Puppies of three weeks can crawl backward as well as forward and will try to walk. Puppies in the transitional phase can move away from the nest to urinate and defecate, and are no longer reliant

on their mother to help them eliminate waste matter from their bodies.

At four weeks of age puppies start teething. Just like human children, puppies have two sets of teeth—a deciduous set is replaced by permanent teeth at around 18 weeks. As soon as the first set of teeth arrives, puppies put things in their mouths to experiment with them—food, objects, each other, and even mom's tail may find their way into a pup's mouth— and play becomes a much more important part of the day.

The arrival of puppy teeth starts the weaning process, where the mother begins to restrict how often and for

left At three weeks old puppies are far more active and are eager to explore.

how long the puppies may suckle. Transitional pups can learn to lap milk from a dish, given the opportunity.

behavioral development

Puppies of three to four weeks start to behave like dogs. Their increased ability to move around means that they can walk and even attempt to run and jump—usually on each other! Pups start to gain control over important aspects of physical communication— they can bark, wag their tails, and bite at each other in play.

Using these essential communication systems takes practice so play begins to take a vital role in the puppies' development. Although the pups still spend a great deal of time sleeping, in the transitional stage their waking hours are spent feeding from their

above At nearly four weeks of age pups begin to play "predatory" games with objects.

mother (when she permits it), feeding from a dish as they begin eating solid food, and playing.

In the wild state, the puppies would move from their original den site to a new, cleaner, and more challenging environment. This is to ensure that predators do not find the pups while they are still vulnerable and increase the puppies' mental and physical stimulation. Some domestic dogs retain this instinct and try to move their puppies in the home.

Contrary to popular belief, adult dogs are not very good at picking up puppies. Rather than carrying them by the back of the neck, as a cat would do, they tend to grab the puppy around the middle, being very careful not to put any pressure on them with their teeth. Some mothers even drag their pups by a hind leg, rather then picking them up, giving them a very bumpy ride!

This behavior dispels the myth that dogs discipline pups by shaking them by the scruff of the neck. Shaking any animal indicates that the dog is trying to kill it, not discipline it, so shaking a puppy to punish it is highly inappropriate. Instead, dams teach their pups discipline through the process of weaning—and being ignored. To a social animal, this is a much more effective punishment and one that humans can copy without fear of harming the puppy.

right *Vision and hearing are fully functional at three weeks. This puppy looks bright and alert.*

action time!

Even at this stage of their development, the puppies are learning a great deal. One of the most important ways that they do this is by watching and imitating their mother. This means that if the mother is anxious or aggressive, the pups could learn to be this way, too. If she is calm, friendly, and relaxed, the pups are likely to behave similarly. Choosing a puppy from a mother who is happy for visitors to see, handle, and pick up her offspring is therefore essential.

Puppies learn a great deal through playing with each other and exploring their environment. During the transitional phase aspects of their habitat can be made more challenging by adding toys, objects to climb on and fall over, and even textured surfaces, so that the puppies become accustomed to walking on different kinds of flooring.

Puppies of this age are rather clumsy and often slide on slippery surfaces, fall off the lowest platform, and tumble into each other in play. This kind of

above As the puppies grow older maternal displays like this become infrequent.

experience helps to give puppies confidence in themselves through "emotional toughening." Puppies who are not permitted to romp around in this normal, natural way may grow into inhibited or anxious adults.

Handling is very important to transitional puppies. They need to have contact with people—and lots of them—if they are to become well-adjusted and confident dogs. Adults and children of all types should be encouraged to see the pups and play with them from this stage onward. Sadly, all too many puppies lead a sheltered life and then show fear of unknown people when they are adult dogs.

In a domestic environment, most puppies are automatically exposed to the many different sounds of daily life. This is essential to prevent a pup growing up fearful of unexpected or unusual sounds. Hearing human voices, in person and on TV and radio, ensures that the noises people make are familiar, while listening to the sounds of washing machines, vacuum cleaners, the clattering of kitchen utensils, and so on help the puppy to adjust to his new home.

4–8 weeks:
the socialization phase

This is the most important phase for creating relationships. In one study, Chihuahua puppies were raised with kittens between the ages of four and eight weeks. These pups were found to prefer the company of cats after this time, and didn't seem to recognize their own species when exposed to other dogs!

below *Dogs learn how to communicate with each other through play.*

This research has strong implications for the way we raise dogs. Puppies need to be handled by many different people in order to form social bonds with humans. They also need to play with members of their own species—singleton pups may miss out if they do not have canine companionship.

physical growth

Bodily changes are highly apparent in the socialization phase. Puppies grow a great amount and begin to look robust

and strong. Refinements to facial expressions and ear positions are seen—and pups begin to use them to communicate with their littermates and mother.

Weaning usually starts at four to five weeks of age, although this depends on the breed and the size of the litter that the mother has had to maintain. Feeding puppies drains the dam's energy and by this time many mothers look like they need a holiday! Weaning is designed to encourage pups to start

to find their own food, which means learning to eat solids. Lapping liquid foods from a dish is usually the first part of this process—and a messy one until pups have got the gist of it! Not long after, puppies will take solid food from a dish and try to eat it—although many can be justly accused of playing with their food!

Weaning is not only a nutritional process: Pups need to learn that they cannot always have their mother's milk whenever they demand it, and this is their first lesson in frustration and restraint (see page 53–54). Research has shown that puppies who are taken away from their mother and littermates too early may never learn this vital lesson, and may grow up to be difficult or problem pets.

behavioral development

It is thought that around five weeks of age, a pup's brainwaves are the same as those of an adult, meaning that even though their stamina and concentration span is limited, their capacity for learning is not. This means that coming when called for food, learning how to communicate with other littermates, and learning from Mom are all possible.

During the socialization stage, the puppy is like a little sponge, absorbing all the information that it is exposed to. Research has shown that cognitive beings who are given a lot of mental stimulation when young are much more likely to have good problem-solving and creative minds in adult life. The more a puppy can learn now, the better! Even in sleep, the pup's brain is active—as puppies can be seen to dream from about five weeks' onward—although what they dream about will always remain a mystery!

right *At six weeks old Holly the puppy already looks like a small adult.*

By now, most puppies are beginning to practice the kinds of behaviors they will need as adults. Puppies of four to five weeks can growl, chase moving objects, shake objects as if killing them, and play rough games with each other, during which they begin learning how to inhibit the strength of their biting.

Pups of both sexes also engage in mounting behavior in the socialization phase. This is not necessarily sexual, but is more an opportunity to practice a social body posture in play.

action time!
Behavioral intervention at this stage in the pups' development is almost entirely up to the breeder. Most puppies stay with their mother, in the breeder's home, until they are seven to eight weeks of age. This is a critical time, during which the pups need to be handled by as many different people as possible to become used to the smell and touch of humans.

Some breeders worry about introducing infection through handling, but the risk is minimal compared to the problems associated with a lack of socialization. Basic hygiene—washing hands before and after handling the pups—is all that is required to keep them safe and yet offer them the chance to develop their social skills.

above *Here a puppy is watched over by a ghost image of itself as an adult.*

early vaccination
New scientific advances mean that puppies can receive early vaccinations to prevent the risk of infection. The early programs usually require the first injection at six weeks and the second at ten weeks. The puppy can then go out and meet the world earlier than with the old regime, where vaccinations were given at eight and 12 weeks.

Puppies also need to take in as many sights and experiences as possible. A litter of four- to eight-week-old pups can be incredibly messy and it is understandable when a breeder chooses to reduce this by keeping them in a kennel or pen for the majority of the time. However, pups need to feel different surfaces underfoot, see different sights, and have as wide a social experience as possible.

All puppies of this age should be given plenty of space and the chance to move away from their bed area to go to the toilet. House training can be very difficult with a puppy who has not had this chance to utilize its natural instincts to be clean.

Ideally, breeders should introduce puppies to all sorts of household and environmental stimuli at this age—even putting the pups in the car and taking them for a short ride helps them to acclimatize to unusual experiences. Meeting vaccinated, friendly adult dogs is a big bonus.

Most important, a short period of individual handling for each puppy every day means that they become used to being with people rather than depending on the company of their littermates and mother. This prepares them for leaving home.

below *The great outdoors offers many new experiences.*

mealtimes

Feeding several puppies at the same time can be a gloriously messy affair. However, it is very important that the breeder supervises mealtimes and makes sure that each puppy has their share. Individual feeding dishes are far better than one large platter, as sharing food can increase competition between puppies and sometimes leads to food-guarding behavior when pups go to their new home.

8–12 weeks:
further socialization

physical growth

By six or seven weeks of age, weaning is normally complete and puppies are increasingly active and independent. The pups' limbs should be sturdy and beginning to develop muscle, their appetites healthy, and their eyes full of inquisitive mischief. Puppies can run, jump, and trot, just like adult dogs, although their stamina and strength is still developing.

Young joints can be accidentally put under stress in the second period of socialization—care must be taken not to over-exercise puppies under the age of nine months, to avoid joint problems later. Excessive stair-climbing or repeated standing on the hind legs are also best avoided.

Sexual behavior is often practiced by puppies in this age group. Male pups' testicles should have descended. Some will mount inanimate objects to "practice" thrusting movements, and may even try this with unsuspecting owners! Distracting the pup and giving him something to chew or play with is the best option.

left *Most adult dogs are kind and gentle with puppies.*

if you have an older dog at home

Allow your older dog to "scold" the puppy if he is being too rough. This should not involve any physical harm to your pup, but should teach him to be more respectful.

Give the older dog more privileges than your puppy to maintain the status quo.

Keep all play between your older dog and pup controlled and supervised. Intervene and have "time out" if it becomes too rough—especially if the older pet is very placid and will allow the puppy to bully.

Take your puppy out without the older dog at least as often as you walk them together. Some puppies learn to rely on their older friends for support and then cannot cope without them.

behavioral development

At eight to 12 weeks puppies are usually into everything! Their desire to explore can get them into trouble if not supervised and their need to chew can be hazardous if not carefully directed onto appropriate chew toys. Their needle-sharp teeth are used to explore objects and other animals—including us!

This biting behavior is completely normal and should be regarded as a valuable part of the pup's education, as he is learning how hard he can bite living creatures, through the process of "bite inhibition" (see page 58). This essential process starts in the litter through play-biting other puppies, but many pups miss out on further education with other dogs until they have finished their vaccination programs at the age of 12–14 weeks. This is a great loss to the pup's behavioral development and needs to be

below *Good socialization and habituation allow dogs to discover the world.*

left Prevent food-guarding by dropping extra treats in the dish while the dog is feeding.

behavior to display toward adult dogs. Trying this behavior in the park, the bullying puppy will probably be strongly reprimanded by a strange dog; this can set up a fear of unknown dogs, which can later lead to aggression toward them. Puppies of between eight and 12

> ### if you are concerned about exposure to disease
>
> - Inquire at your veterinary surgery about early vaccination. Some programs finish at 10 weeks so puppies can go straight out
> - Carry your puppy out and about. Although this experience is not the same as walking around, it is a good compromise
> - Visit friends and family, taking your puppy into their homes for wider social experiences
> - Visit friendly, vaccinated adult dogs in their own homes or yards. Vaccinated dogs present no risks of infection
> - Have a puppy party! Invite friends and relatives to your home to meet the new pet
> - Take the puppy for car rides. Seeing the world from a moving vehicle is very different to experiencing it for real, but it accustoms the pet to motor travel
> - Find out whether your veterinary surgery holds puppy parties. These usually offer puppies the chance to socialize between the first and second vaccination. All play between pups should be friendly and controlled

compensated for as much as possible. Early vaccination and a good puppy class help to overcome this deprivation.

action time!
As it is usual for puppies to move to their new home at between seven and eight weeks of age, the continued socialization and behavioral development of the puppy is up to his or her new owner.

Some puppies are brought into a new home where a dog is already present. This can have advantages and disadvantages for your pup's behavioral welfare. While the presence of an older

dog may help your puppy to feel more secure and comfortable at first, substantial evidence exists to show that a large proportion of dogs that show aggression to other dogs later in life were a "second dog" that grew up with an older animal at home.

One of the reasons for this may be that a placid older dog will let a new puppy get away with substantial amounts of rough play and bullying. If the older dog allows the play to get out of control, or allows the puppy to dominate him, without using any canine discipline, the puppy can think this is acceptable weeks of age should go out into the world to meet as many different people, dogs, and other animals as much as possible. Waiting for the pup's vaccinations to be complete is too late, so make sure you do as much as possible between the ages of eight and 12 weeks. Habituation—familiarity with the environment—is also critical, so follow the advice on pages 48–51 to ensure your puppy does not miss out.

breed characteristics

Around this time it is usually possible to spot inherent breed or type characteristics in the pups' behavior. For example, it is usually between eight and 12 weeks that terrier puppies start to show an interest in chasing and digging, retrievers want to pick up objects and carry them, and herding breeds start to give "eye" to moving objects and animals—all in preparation for their roles later in life.

below *Ask you veterinarian which innoculations your puppy will need.*

12–18 weeks: the juvenile phase

physical growth

From around ten weeks onward, puppies are heading into the juvenile period. Development and behavioral maturity now depend very heavily on the breed and individual. Indeed, small fast-maturing breeds, such as some of the smaller terriers, often have most of their adult behaviors and physical attributes by the time they are 16 weeks old, while slow-maturing breeds, such as Newfoundlands, may still look and behave like immature puppies.

behavioral development

Most puppies go through a "fear period" at 12–18 weeks. Until then, most puppies show little fear of their surroundings, other dogs, or humans, especially if they have been well socialized until this point. However, for many puppies anxiety suddenly appears and they show fear of objects or events that they were completely comfortable with only the day or week before!

This phase can be explained by looking at the dog's wild ancestry. In a wild pack, a litter of puppies stays close to the den site with at least one or two adults to keep them safe and supervise them, even if the rest of the pack is away hunting. Suddenly, puppies are much more mobile and very confident. They may even wander off by themselves to explore or play. Suddenly becoming fearful of novel stimuli or new experiences at this stage therefore keeps them safe; they are more likely to run away from a dog or animal that they have never met before than approach it.

While this phase is perfectly normal, it can cause considerable worry to new owners and needs to be handled in the correct manner if the pup's fear is not to become established. If your puppy shows fear of any new or even familiar person, dog, object, or circumstance, try to ignore the behavior as much as

right *This Border Collie pup learns how to interact with his "uncle."*

left *As puppies become independent, play with toys increases.*

possible. It may be tempting to reassure the pup, to stroke him and talk to him, but this should be avoided at all costs: your puppy will not understand your words, but may think that he is being praised for being fearful!

It is far better to simply be patient and wait. After a period of time where the puppy realizes his fear has brought no response, he will become more confident again. At this point you should praise and reward bravery.

Officially the end of puppyhood, 18 weeks sees the loss of the puppy's deciduous teeth and the setting in of permanent teeth. This can cause teething troubles similarly to those seen in human babies, such as sore gums, irritability, and the need to soothe the mouth by chewing. Chew toys can be stored in the fridge to keep them cool.

action time: attachment

From the age of around four weeks, puppies learn to form social attachments. Once your puppy has been in the home and living as part of your family for a week or two, it is likely that he or she will have bonded with you very closely. This is why we keep dogs—their loyalty to us means that we form bonds with them in return.

However, during this time there is a risk that a puppy may become over-dependent on one or more members of the household. This can cause all kinds of problems, the most common of which is a condition known as separation anxiety. This describes the emotional state of a dog who cannot cope when his owner is not present.

Dogs with separation problems howl, whine, or bark when left alone. They may lose control of their bowels and mess indoors, or they can become destructive, chewing, scratching, or shredding objects, door frames, or furnishings in an attempt to follow their owner or to relieve their distress. To prevent separation problems, it is sensible to teach your puppy to behave calmly when left alone for short periods and become partly independent from you.

At this stage, puppies are at their most malleable and eager to please. This means that the majority of their basic training needs to be done before the age of 18 weeks. (See pages 56–63 and 108–119.)

teaching your puppy to cope alone

- Do not allow the puppy to be your "shadow" when you are at home. Shut doors between you regularly and routinely, so that the pup cannot always have contact with you
- Give attention when you choose, rather than when your pup demands it
- Make sure your puppy is tired and has been to the toilet before you leave him
- Feeding your puppy will make him more sleepy and restful
- Leave your puppy with the radio on and a really enjoyable chew toy. A "Kong" stuffed with food or rawhide bone is ideal
- Leave quickly and quietly. Do not fuss over your pup before leaving
- Leave your pup for only a few minutes to begin with, then build up the time to an hour or so
- On your return, be matter-of-fact. Take your puppy into the yard to relieve himself right away. Do not scold him for going to the toilet indoors in your absence
- Practice leaving your pup by himself for short periods, frequently. Your pup is at greatest risk of experiencing separation problems if you have taken him home after the age of eight weeks or if you spend all your time together

left *Basic training helps to build the bond between human and dog. Tidbits used as lures help the process.*

right *Puppies need to become accustomed to all kinds of sights, sounds, smells, and experiences.*

5–9 months:
the "teenage" phase

physical growth

By seven months it is perfectly possible for a puppy to have increased his or her birth weight by 15–40 times, depending on the breed. This is a huge increase in a very short space of time. A puppy's nutritional requirements will have reflected this growth rate, but now it is likely that food intake will plateau and the puppy will need less frequent meals, cutting back from four or five meals a day at 12 weeks to only two at six months old.

sexual development

Sexual development progresses in both sexes and this is the time when it is usually most noticeable. Male dogs may begin to lift their legs to urinate. However, this is heavily influenced by the breed, maturity of the individual, and whether the puppy has had the opportunity to imitate an older male dog. It is not uncommon for some bitches to copy male dogs and pass urine in a strange mixture of squatting and leg-cocking positions!

Females may come into season for the first time. In some bitches this can be as early as seven months, in others it may not occur until as late as 14 months. Domestic dogs commonly have two seasons per year. This is the time when a female dog is fertile and can become pregnant if she is mated.

For most bitches, their first season is a little bewildering. Before the season, hormonal changes may affect her mood, and other dogs may start to pester her as she begins to smell more attractive. Signs that your bitch may be coming into season are varied. She may wash herself more frequently and you may notice that her vulva is slightly swollen. Many bitches urinate more frequently before they come into season, often in tiny amounts over a wide area.

behavioral development

This stage can loosely be called the "teenage" part of a pup's behavioral development. Puppies of between five and nine months are often rather awkward, gangly, and clumsy in appearance. They may also attempt to behave as if they are adult dogs, while still appearing very puppy-like in movement and posture.

Many "teenage" dog can be quite exasperating! Males, in particular can

left *Discovering the sea. Puppies need to paddle near the shore before going deeper.*

Unfortunately, this is also the time when training seems to have been forgotten—encouraging your exuberant, adolescent dog to come back when it is called in the park or yard can be a long and trying process!

Overall, much more time and effort is required in training an adolescent dog than is needed to train a puppy. The methods you use should still be kind and gentle, but with more repetition and practice. Recall problems, jumping up, and pulling on the leash are the three most commonly reported training difficulties at this time but all can be solved with time and patience.

You may need to consider neutering now, particularly if your female dog has not had a season and you want her spayed before she has her first.

become driven by their hormonal status, becoming overridden with the effects of testosterone and behaving in an excessively sexual, competitive, or even aggressive manner, particularly toward other dogs. Neutering is a good option for dogs who seem particularly "driven" by this hormonal effect.

action time!

Owners need to be aware that a second socialization phase is required for some young dogs, as they can feel anxious at the sight or presence of adult dogs and may become defensive as a result.

below *Gangly, clumsy, and leggy: signs of the "teenage" stage!*

9–12 months:
reaching maturity

physical growth

By the age of one year, it is possible for a dog to have increased his or her birth weight by 60 times! These are now the months of maturity. Most dogs have reached their full height by this time but are still growing in girth. In males particularly the chest is likely to deepen after this time, and the head is likely to broaden a little, depending on breed characteristics.

Dogs will easily have attained their adult strength by this stage, and although their muscle development tends to be influenced by the amount and type of exercise that they receive, they will be able to control their bodies fully.

Puppies usually grow their adult coat by the time they are seven or eight months of age. This is normally harsher and longer than the fluffy puppy coat, and typically starts as a "saddle" effect on the back, depending on the breed and coat type. However, the full adult coat usually takes up to a year to grow, and this may affect the dog's eventual coloring.

Teeth are fully adult now and are well set into the jawbone. Chewing is still a necessity, and nearly all dogs, no matter their age, continue to enjoy chewing on a bone or toy.

left *As your puppy completes his first year, his adult height is reached.*

behavioral development

After the excitement of the teenage phase most dogs start to settle down. This is partly due to the reduction in hormonal effects—particularly in neutered dogs, who are relieved of their need to compete for a mate, and partly due to the effects of ongoing training.

Calmer behavior is normally seen after a year or so, especially as the dog has built relationships with the family and understands the daily routine. However, it is no surprise that many of the dogs in rescue shelters also fit this age category: Without training and adequate socialization in the early weeks, many year-old dogs are in full possession of strength and energy, but do not know how to behave around humans or other dogs. All dogs need to have their intelligence and exuberance channeled appropriately to prevent them finding their own, usually destructive ways to amuse themselves.

Your dog's character will now be fully formed. Although he or she will still be affected by experiences and events and continue to learn throughout his or her life, your dog's personality and general outlook is here to stay. Attitudes formed as a puppy often have far-reaching effects, so owners are often disappointed that their dog has not "grown out" of certain behaviors that they do not like.

Re-training is possible but it is much harder than teaching a puppy. In the same way that it is much easier for us to learn a foreign language at five years of age than 50, so dogs need more time and patience to re-train or rehabilitate after their first year.

action time!

In many ways, the period after puppyhood is one of the most rewarding times in a dog's life. Your relationship with your dog is well established and you understand his needs, moods, and expressions, yet he is still young, enthusiastic, and keen to learn. Now is the time to consolidate your training with your dog, either through a further training class, or by teaching your pet a new sport or tricks at home.

left *If your pet has not been well socialized by 12 months, he may not allow displays of affection such as this.*

Agility is an exciting sport for dogs and their owners. Dogs are required to learn how to tackle various obstacles, such as jumping through a tire, leaping over hurdles, running through a tunnel, or weaving around a set of poles. A whole course of such obstacles is then completed by the dog as quickly as possible, with instructions and encouragement from the owner.

As agility training involves jumping over hurdles, which might harm the developing bones and muscles of a puppy, this sport is specifically for dogs older than a year. Basic obedience training is needed before taking part in this specialized area, as the dogs are trained off-leash and are likely to come into contact with other dogs and people when practicing.

trick training

If you haven't started to teach your dog tricks, now's the time. For many dogs of this age, mental stimulation is just as important as physical stimulation, so learning new exercises

and tasks will help to keep him occupied. Tricks can be as simple as "give a paw" on command, or as complex as loading and unloading the washing machine! Many dogs are trained using positive and fun methods to perform such jobs for disabled owners, and there is no reason why your dog cannot learn similar tasks.

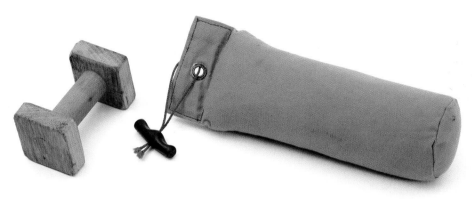

above *These items are used for advanced retrieval training.*

Teaching your dog to bring the newspaper, fetch your slippers, or find the TV remote control are all based on teaching your dog an effective retrieve command, which many dogs have learned by one year of age. Teaching tricks helps you to perfect the behavior your dog has already learned.

Even if you choose not to compete with your dog or teach him new tasks, do not make the mistake of believing that his socialization is complete. Any dog who is deprived of social experiences begins to lose his ability to socially interact—with his own kind and with people. Ongoing socialization is required for the duration of the dog's life.

Over a period of 14–15 years, your dog may be asked to live in a number of places, with different environmental pressures and possibly different people living in the same home. A dog's life can easily span the birth, growth, and school days of children, the arrival of other pets, and the loss of security in the form of a much-loved owner or familiar territory. Prepare your dog for all these changes by making sure he leads as full a life as possible. In return he will offer you security, loyalty, and a constancy that is now rare in other areas of our lives.

left *Agility test are fun and exciting for the young dog and his owner.*

socialization
and the critical period

left *All puppies need to be trained to moderate their biting behavior.*

It may be surprising, but each and every dog that lives with a family needs to be "domesticated" individually. Our pet dogs are descended from wolves, and although they differ in many ways from their truly wild cousins, they have not lost all of the similarities.

Research has shown that puppies who do not have contact with human beings before the end of the critical period grow up to behave like wild dogs. These animals never trust humans, enjoy their company, or learn the basic obedience exercises that make dogs so much easier to live with. Similarly, dogs who have been isolated from the company of other dogs during this period show fear and hostility toward their own kind for the rest of their lives.

Thankfully, the last few years has shown a revolution in understanding how vital this early period is to the

above *Dogs are social animals and even unrelated animals can demonstrate maternal behavior.*

ways dogs develop and behave. It is now known that keeping a puppy isolated from the world, from other puppies and dogs, or people until it is past 12 weeks of age would be like keeping a child in total isolation until he or she was seven or eight years old.

what is socialization?

Socialization has been the buzzword of the dog world in recent years, yet few people understand its full implications. Socialization means learning how to interact with humans, other dogs, and sometimes other pets. Socialization means learning a language and being able to communicate in that language with others—rather than ignoring them or becoming aggressive or defensive.

A well-socialized puppy can read the body language and facial expressions of people and other dogs easily and quickly, and knows how to respond appropriately. This response may be to play with the other being, to be wary of it and keep away, or to approach for contact, such as stroking or nuzzling.

Good socialization also gives the puppy choices. If one communication strategy does not work, the puppy can try another approach. Equally, if the puppy makes a mistake or meets an animal that lacks social skills, he or she can cope with the situation and make a decision that avoids conflict.

rehabilitation beyond the critical period

Puppies learn how to communicate with other beings during a very short period of their development. This period is so important that it is named "the critical period." It lasts between five and 12 weeks of age, and although puppies continue to learn after this time, their whole outlook is affected by their experience and patterns of learning during this period.

Individuals exist that may have had inadequate amounts of socialization during the critical period, yet make good pets later on. Puppies born and raised in a kennel at the bottom of a yard or in a barn may have only met one or two people in their whole lives until they move to a new home at eight weeks, then have to catch up quickly with their new surroundings and contact with humans if they are to cope as a pet dog.

Thankfully, such puppies often recover, and with careful and controlled rehabilitation can make up for some of their lost time and opportunity. However, whether they ever reach their full potential as confident, outgoing, and self-assured individuals is doubtful. It is always advisable to buy a puppy from a breeder that understands the importance of early socialization, and to quickly seek help from a behavior specialist if you feel that your puppy had a deprived start and now needs extra "homework" to be able to catch up.

socializing your puppy

The most vital help that you can give your puppy to ensure that they are well socialized during the critical period is to ensure that they get out to meet the world! Puppies desperately need to meet and mix with as many different people and dogs as possible to fluently communicate and understand body language. From a pup's perspective, all people look, smell, and sound very different, so while a socially inexperienced puppy could be completely familiar with you and other members of your family, he may become a quivering wreck when meeting someone new.

understanding human body language

Interpreting human body language and facial expressions takes time and practice for all puppies. For example, puppies need to know that when humans smile, they often show their teeth. In dog language, this is extremely threatening—bared teeth imply that the dog is using aggression to keep someone away and will attack if they do not leave. Puppy need to understand that it means the opposite when humans show their teeth.

Equally, most people attempt to greet a puppy by extending their hand and trying to touch him or her on the head. In canine language, this is extremely bad manners! A paw on the head usually means that the other dog is attempting

below *Socialization should invlove all sorts of animal, as well as people.*

to dominate the puppy and is regarded as highly threatening—yet we are only trying to be friendly! Without many repetitions of these meetings, puppies do not have the opportunity to discover that humans are good to be around.

variety is the spice of life

It is important to realize that puppies view the world differently to people. A human being sitting down and reading a book looks completely different to someone standing up with their hands on their head. Can you imagine what most puppies make of people wearing glasses on the first few occasions that they see them? What about people wearing hats? To a puppy, a human being wearing a crash helmet may look like a being from outer space,

while children who have been to a carnival and have had their faces painted must be totally unrecognizable! Puppies need to be exposed to these kinds of visual experiences in order to discover that no matter how human beings look, they are safe to be with.

In the same way, puppies need to find out that all dogs are dogs. This may seem obvious, but a puppy from a pedigree litter will only ever have met dogs that look like him. Imagine his surprise the first time that he meets a dog that looks nothing like his mother or littermates—particularly if it is very different in coloring, coat length, or size. It will take many, many meetings for an average German Shepherd puppy to discover that Saint Bernards, Hungarian Pulis, and even Chihuahuas are dogs, too!

to help your puppy become familiar with other people, other dogs, and other pets, he or she needs to meet and mix with as many of these as possible:

Adults of different ages
Children of different ages
People of different nationalities
People wearing different clothing, such as hats, glasses, and gloves
Men with beards
Dogs of different ages, breeds, sizes, and colors
Pets, such as cats, horses, rabbits, and guinea pigs

socialization classes, benefits and rules

A well-run puppy socialization class can offer some of the most beneficial lessons in life a puppy can have. Socialization classes enable puppies to meet and mix with pups of a similar age, as well as have an opportunity to be handled by many different people, including children. For many owners, finding enough members of the opposite sex, children, or other dogs is almost impossible before the end of the critical period—and this is where a class situation helps enormously. However, a good class should also offer owners the chance to learn how to train their puppies, build a good relationship with them, and prevent problems occurring in the future.

Unfortunately, when puppy classes were first launched, some instructors allowed the class to consist of an hour's free play, without any intervention or training. This led to some puppies being bullied by bigger, stronger, or more confident pups; the victims became more anxious and the bullies learned to enjoy bullying other dogs— a recipe for disaster!

Now it is understood that a good puppy class needs to offer a combination of controlled play and fun, gentle training. The pups' owners always need to be the most important factor in the dogs' lives and these relationships should be built on, not undermined. Play between puppies needs to be carefully monitored, to ensure that the right behaviors are

above Puppies should learn appropriate behaviors at socialization classes—aggression is not one of them!

what should a puppy class offer?

● Puppies of a similar age—under 18 weeks—to play with and improve socialization
● An experienced instructor who can help with training and behavioral difficulties
● Other owners who are prepared to help socialize each others' pups, just by being there, through handling and petting
● A warm and friendly atmosphere, so that everyone can enjoy the experience
● A safe environment so that dogs and owners can be relaxed and enjoy controlled, off-leash play

being learned, and all the pups should practice appropriate communication between themselves and their owners, as well as their playmates.

Ask your veterinary surgeon to recommend a puppy class. In the USA and many European countries the Association of Pet Dog Trainers can help you to find a good class by locating the nearest member, who is assessed and accredited according to a strict code of practice.

left Body language and social skills are easily learnt with a friend of the same age.

interpreting play behavior

A useful lesson that puppy trainers can teaches owners is how to understand dog body language. Some of the more common poses in play include:

Play bow: The puppy puts his head and front legs low to the ground and his bottom and tail high in the air, as if he is going to pounce. This shows an intention to play and is often copied by the other dog.

Paw raises: The puppy raises his paw in a floppy-elbowed fashion, pawing at the air, or sometimes even patting the other dog. This is a clear play signal that indicates the puppy means no harm.

Bounces: Some puppies will bounce, so that both front feet pounce toward another puppy. Pups sometimes bounce, then run away as an invitation to be chased.

Hip swings: Larger breeds in particular, such as German Shepherd Dogs, like to sidle up to other pups then spin around quickly, knocking the other animal gently with their hips. Turning his back shows that the hip-swinging pup means no harm.

Hackles up: Puppies often raise the hair on the back of the neck—the hackles—if they are unsure of themselves at the start of a play session. This does not indicate aggression, but insecurity and excitement. On the whole, this should be ignored—the hackles soon subside as the pup grows in confidence.

communicating
with other dogs

One of the most important facets of a pup's development before the end of the critical period, and certainly before the age of about 16 weeks, is how to communicate with members of his or her own species. Dogs have a special language that they use to understand and interpret what they are saying to each other. This needs to be learned before adolescence—young animals have "puppy license" and can get away with behaving inappropriately and immaturely, but are expected to know how to communicate with other dogs by the time they become sexually mature.

eyes

It is an interesting fact that no matter what the mammalian species, a direct stare is nearly always interpreted as a threat. This is certainly true for dogs, who quickly need to learn that averting their gaze when greeting a new dog is a cautious action that will keep them out of trouble. Their mother will have started to teach them this in the litter, by staring hard at them when they behaved in an inappropriate way, then following the stare with a snap or growl, if necessary.

ears

Ear positions are important to dogs. Unfortunately, the messages that these give are often confused by man's interference, as some dogs have been bred to have long, pendulous, and almost immobile ears. However, in breeds that have highly mobile, upright ears, the messages that they carry are clearly visible. For example, ears pointed upright and forward show that the dog is alert and ready for action; ears held back or pinned to the head show that the dog is in a high state of anxiety or fear.

body posture

Puppies very often assume a low body posture if they feel threatened or uncertain in a new situation. This is an attempt to make themselves as small as

left *Turning the face away clearly indicates the puppy presents no threat.*

possible so that they can sneak away or hide. Typically, a dog who is very fearful crouches low to the ground and tucks its tail right between its legs.

tail positions and wags

Tails are vital to the dog's communication systems. Man's intervention has made this more difficult for those breeds who have their tails docked (amputated) at an early age. In dogs with natural tails, the angle of the tail and its movement gives information about how that individual is feeling and what his intentions are. A wagging tail does not always show happiness. A tail held high and wagging vigorously shows confidence and even aggression, while a tail held low and gently wagging may show uncertainty. Dogs which tuck their tails right underneath them are showing anxiety.

right A puppy's first lessons in canine communication come from playing with their mother and littermates.

movement

Watching dogs freely interact is fascinating and teaches a great deal about canine body language. Most dogs, if greeting each other for the first time, are careful to avoid full eye contact and approach each other in a "banana" curve, rather than a straight line. This shows the other dog that the stranger means no harm and is non-

above Scent messages are as important as body language, such as tail position.

aggressive. It also explains why many puppies try to curve away from another dog if it is approaching—pulling sideways on the leash in an attempt to show clear body language that it is non-threatening.

habituation

Habituation is the smart word for familiarity. No matter what breed or type, all puppies need to become familiar with the sights, sounds, and smells of a domestic home. Every pup needs to have grown used to seeing the washing machine and vacuum cleaner and hearing all of the sounds of a busy household well before the critical age of 12 weeks.

Before this time, puppies are keen to explore—they approach rather than avoid new stimuli and are curious about everything in their environment. However, after 12 weeks, puppies start to develop fear responses to the sight of unknown objects and unfamiliar sounds. This means that they move away from novel stimuli, rather than moving forward to explore.

Inevitably, much of this "social training" needs to occur while your puppy is still with his breeder. This means that well before you collect your puppy, he needs to have been exposed to a wide variety of domestic stimuli. Before they leave the nest puppies need to have seen and been handled by a range of men, women, and children, who look, smell, and sound different to one another. They should have become accustomed to hearing such noises as the television, radio, and hair dryer. They even need to have walked on

left *Home away from home; traveling crates can be very useful.*

different types of surface textures: grass, smooth or slippery flooring, concrete, carpet, and earth. Ideally, they will also have been exposed to the movements and smells of everyday human life: people walking, running, and sitting, being taken out in the car, and carried around—all before you take him home.

Sadly, many puppies miss out on this essential facet of their development. Pups born in a barn or kennel no matter how clean they are will have missed out and it can be difficult to rehabilitate animals that have had a deprived start. No matter what start your puppy had, there is no time to lose once he is at home. Even if your puppy has not finished his vaccination

above *Exporing the big, wide world can be daunting at six weeks old.*

program, you can get your puppy out and about to meet the world—and invite the world into your home to meet your pup, too! Carrying your puppy offers some compromise between the risk of infection and the benefits of socialization. Meeting vaccinated adult dogs and puppies is perfectly safe, so ask friends and relatives if you can visit with your pup as soon as possible.

familiarity breeds success
Exposure to people, animals, objects, and situations needs to be so frequent

that the puppy ignores them. For example, the first time that a puppy sees an umbrella being put up, he may react fearfully. However, when he's seen it happen dozens of times it's so uneventful that he will ignore it. This needs to occur with every kind of stimuli imaginable. Baby carriages, bicycles, hats, walking sticks, glasses, traffic, washing machines, and vacuum cleaners are good examples of non-living items that your puppy will need to have been exposed to before the end of the critical period.

Think about what kinds of animal your pup will be likely to meet in your local area in the future. If you live near the countryside, how do you want him to react when he sees sheep, for example? Do you want him to interact with them? No matter how friendly he may be, this could be misinterpreted by the farmer! For most pet dogs it is far better that they simply ignore common livestock such

---

habituation checklist

Before 12 weeks of age your puppy needs to become familiar with:

● **Sights:** baby carriages, bicycles, traffic cones and road signs, horses, sheep, cats, people wearing hats, carrying umbrellas
● **Sounds:** washing machines, vacuum cleaners, hair dryers, car engines, air brakes, trains, shopping carts
● **Scents:** the veterinarian's waiting room, dog toothpaste, perfume, farm animals
● **Touch:** being handled by people such as the veterinarian and children, grooming

as sheep, ducks, chickens, cattle, and horses. This can only be achieved if the puppy sees them so frequently that he begins to regard them as tedious. Taking a good book and sitting in the rain by fields of sheep and cattle may be the only option!

Every waking second of every day, dogs are learning. We know that it is much easier for someone to learn a new language, for example, when they are a child, and the same can be said of

dogs. Enrolling in a puppy socialization class will help to teach you the techniques and understanding to be able to train your dog effectively, right from the start, but is still no substitute for as much exposure to the outside world as you can arrange.

watch yourself!

All new experiences have the capacity to create fear. If your puppy shows anxiety when seeing, hearing, or touching something new, make sure that your reaction does not compound the fear and create a long-term problem. Look away, fold your arms,

and say nothing, rather than attempting to reassure a worried puppy. It is human nature to want to comfort a frightened animal, but this can be misinterpreted as a reward for the behavior and the emotion behind it. Dogs cannot understand spoken language—and this means that even a well-intentioned "There's a good dog, you'll be fine" may be misinterpreted as "Good dog for being scared!" To ensure that your puppy grows into a confident adult dog, allow him to overcome fear in his own time, then praise and reward brave behavior, rather than fearful responses.

below *Puppies need to learn their physical limits in the outside world.*

weaning:
its **behavioral** importance

For the first month of life, puppies are entirely dependent on their mother's milk for their nutritional needs. Most bitches stay with their litter for the majority of the day and night and roll onto one side to expose their teats to allow the pups to suckle at will. As the weeks pass, the bitch will start to leave the nest site for short periods and will only feed on her return.

At around four to five weeks of age, puppies start to become independent from their mother. They are increasingly active—and are able to walk, play, and explore their environment. At this time, they need to learn to be nutritionally independent too—taking solid food in place of their mother's milk. The mother is the one to instigate this important process—she usually has to insist that puppies make the move from milk bar to dish!

The timing of this change ensures that the dam does not relinquish too much of her bodily reserves, which would put her survival at risk. Weaning is triggered by the pain suckling causes the dam. When the puppies' first, needle-sharp teeth begin to grow through the gums, there can be little

doubt that suckling eight or nine pups must be distinctly uncomfortable!

Up to this point, all the puppies were able to suckle from their mother on demand, and later every time she returned to the nest after a short absence. Suddenly, the rules change. The bitch spends longer amounts of time away from the puppies, making her the target of a mob of hungry pups on her return.

After a while, most bitches tend to get up and walk away from pups who try and get a drink when they have not been invited. This often leaves puppies to literally drop off the bitch's teats. This has an interesting effect on the pups, who become frustrated and try even harder to reach their mother and latch on. As they try harder to get to her, the bitch needs to redirect their demands for food to another source—her mouth in a wild situation, where she would regurgitate food, and a bowl of food in our domestic setting.

left *Border Collie pups converge on a milk dish in an early stage of weaning.*

right *Milk teeth are small, pointed, and very sharp.*

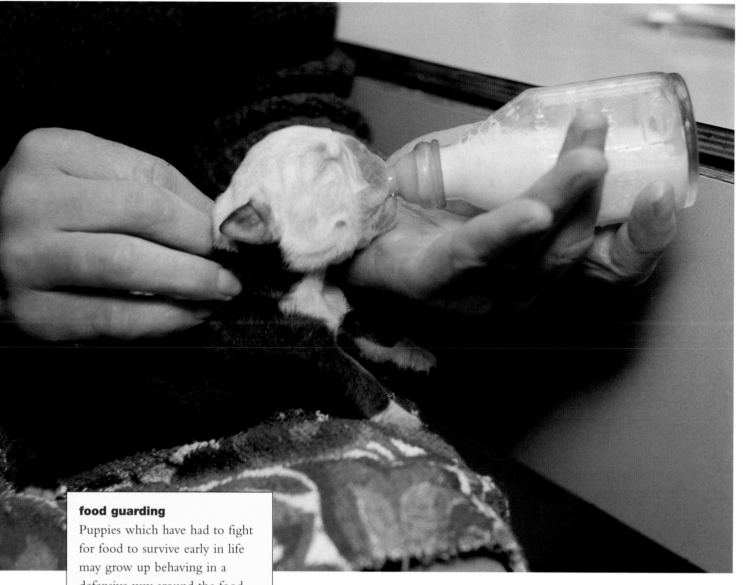

above *Hand-reared puppies need special behavioral care.*

food guarding

Puppies which have had to fight for food to survive early in life may grow up behaving in a defensive way around the food bowl. Ideally, breeders should give puppies several dishes from which to feed, particularly if the litter is large and competition for food is high.

Puppies only guard their food if they fear it is being threatened. To correct this behavior, don't take your pup's food bowl away while he or she is eating; instead, only approaching the eating pup to drop in extra goodies by hand. If these extras are even more delicious than the food he is already eating, he will soon learn to enjoy your proximity to the bowl and look forward to having you approach him during mealtimes.

Until the pups realize they should eat their first solid food, good mothers show their displeasure at puppies' repeated attempts to feed in firm but gentle ways. A hard stare is the pups' first warning. A growl may follow. Very persistent puppies may be subjected to a nose-butt, where they are pushed firmly away, or even an inhibited snap, where the bitch snaps her jaws close to the puppy without making contact.

Puppies are not born with an innate knowledge of what a hard stare or even a growl means. Such signals come to have meaning when associated with the denial of a reward, and this is the pups' first experience of social discipline.

Sensitive puppies work out the meanings of these gestures very quickly and soon give up trying to feed if their mother gives them that "look." More determined puppies, however, may push their mother to the limit and require her to be 100 percent consistent in her signaling. Eventually, all the puppies learn that when their mother returns to them they need to lick her around the mouth and face, rather than her underbelly, to solicit food and attention. In the wild state, mothers then give their puppies "weaning food" of regurgitated meat. In our domestic setting it is up to the breeder to provide solid food for puppies—this is one of the reasons why pups relate so well to people and come running when the breeder calls. However, it is interesting that nearly all dogs retain the basic greeting behaviors learned as a tiny puppy and greet other dogs and people by sniffing and even licking at their faces.

This essential lesson in communication teaches the pups to resolve conflict with other animals, humans, and even the environment. It gives them a coping strategy for later in life when not everything will go their way—they may become frustrated, but soon resort to resignation.

The behavioral effects of weaning also have an impact on a puppy's ability to learn the meaning of other dogs' body language—in effect, how to "speak dog." Puppies need to learn to recognize signals from other dogs that tell them to calm or stop their behavior. Later this ensures that the puppy does not overstep the mark with other adult dogs and that he is able to use these signals himself.

right *In the first stage of weaning the mother walks away, denying the pups food.*

social rules

Dogs are social creatures, so just like us, they respond to social order and social rules. Very few dogs can be considered to be dominant—and certainly no puppy can be classed in this way, as dominance is related to reproduction and the perpetuation of genes! However, some dogs, particularly bright ones, can become opportunistic, and given an inch try to take a mile!

Just like children, dogs appreciate being given boundaries in which to fit their behavior. Puppies do not have a sense of right and wrong, they can only understand what is rewarding and what is not, so establishing and maintaining sensible house rules from the start can save much confusion and conflict later on.

house rules

House rules will vary from owner to owner and dog to dog. Some easy-going breeds, types, or individuals may need very few, while strong-minded willful animals need more. Overall, try to start as you mean to go on. It is very unfair to allow your puppy to sleep on your bed for the first three months and then decide that because he is too big and heavy he should be banished to the floor!

left *Dogs need to learn when to be quiet and calm.*

right *Feed your pup from his bowl, not the table.*

1. Sleeping arrangements

Decide where you want your pup to sleep and stick with it. Most puppies are better off in the kitchen in their own bed or basket. If you decide to have your puppy in the bedroom with you, provide somewhere on the floor for him to rest—the middle of the duvet may well cause domestic disputes between spouses and can lead to frayed tempers if the dog comes in from the yard with muddy paws!

2. Eating time

Make a rule that no one feeds the puppy from the table. This is simply a practical and hygiene matter. No one appreciates being stared at while eating, let alone having a dog drool copiously while they switch their gaze between you and your food. Once started this is a difficult habit to stop, so be firm from the outset.

It is also sensible to ensure that your dog does not become too fussy about his own food. Some puppies train their owners to buy a different kind of food every week—simply by refusing to eat what is put in front of them, they can make their owner offer them something different!

3. Attention games

Nearly all puppies enjoy receiving attention and affection from their owners—and rightly so. However, having a dog constantly interrupt work, conversations with visitors, or a restful evening in front of the TV can be highly irritating. Some attention-seeking dogs are so clever that they work on new behaviors that their owners can't ignore—such as barking at them, stealing household items, or, in extreme cases, using aggression. Again, prevention is better than cure and ignoring your puppy on occasions when you are busy and not ready to give attention is a sensible approach. Turning away, averting eye contact, and remaining silent gives your pup the message, "Not right now."

4. Freedom of movement

There may be areas of your house that you would prefer to have as dog-free zones. If this is the case, put up a baby-gate or shut the door to prevent your puppy from going into this area to begin with. Dogs do not need to be with us constantly and can suffer over-attachment problems if they are, so start as you mean to go on.

The rules you make for your puppy should be tailored to your individual needs. However, once decided, make sure the whole family knows the rules and follows them. Many behavioral problems in adult dogs can be attributed to a lack of clear signals of reward and non-reward, or rules, which leads the dog to test the boundaries of social behavior.

bite inhibition

From only a few weeks old, puppies are armed with a set of formidable teeth and jaws that are incredibly strong in comparison to their size. Obviously, these are not for hunting and killing prey—as the pup would not be ready to go out on such expeditions for several months—so what are they for? The answer is simple: these sharp little teeth are designed to hurt!

Biting during play is essential and normal for all puppies, and almost as soon as pups are mobile, they start to engage in rough-and-tumble games with their littermates. They also start to explore the world—and a big part of this consists of putting objects into their mouth to see what they taste and feel like, as well as finding out whether they are living or dead! This is done by biting the object and seeing whether it reacts or not—those sharp teeth will certainly hurt if the subject is alive!

Puppy-biting teaches a pup just how hard it can bite other living things. Clearly, it can exert a huge amount of pressure on a lifeless object such as a toy without causing any kind of reaction, while trying the same behavior on a littermate—or on Mom—will most certainly result in a big response!

above *Older dogs soon tell puppies when their bites begin to hurt.*

Watching puppies play together makes this obvious. They play by biting each other's ears, tail, legs, and any other part they can latch onto. This is accepted quite happily—until the pressure becomes too hard. Then the "victim" is likely to yelp and stop playing for a short while, leaving the biting pup to realize there were consequences to his actions. This process is known as bite inhibition and it is vital that all puppies learn how to moderate their bites before they lose their deciduous teeth at around 18 weeks of age.

teaching further inhibition
In our homes, pups continue to learn about how hard they can bite by practicing on us. This is normal and should not be treated as aggression. However, it is not acceptable for dogs to bite people, and puppies need to be given education in how to moderate their biting with humans, too.

Because pups understand what a yelp means, communicating that you are hurt, rather than angry when bitten, is highly effective. Each and every time your puppy mouths your hands or clothes, you should yelp loudly or give a shout, then turn away as if to nurse your wounds. Your puppy will probably look a little bewildered and should stop, but only temporarily. It usually takes several weeks for the puppy to realize that he cannot put any pressure on you at all, then you can yelp even if he puts his mouth on you gently, finally teaching him that he cannot initiate biting.

This vital process works well for the vast majority of puppies. However, there are two exceptions: pups who are already over 14 weeks old and puppies who have learned to bite for attention.

If you find that yelping and turning away has had no effect, despite total consistency in the family for two

above *Bite inhibition gradually reduces the pressure the puppy uses.*

weeks, or if your puppy seems to become more excited and snappy if you yelp and turn away, you may need a different strategy. This involves taking all the fun out of the behavior. As soon as your dog puts his mouth on you, even in play, immediately expel him to the kitchen, or behind a door or baby gate in another room. This social isolation should only last about three minutes, then he can rejoin the family. However, he must be put away each time that he bites. Total consistency is required if the biting is not to become a habit that will be even harder to break later on.

A good, well-controlled puppy socialization class can help your puppy to develop bite inhibition. Seek help early if you experience problems in this area.

how **puppies** learn

Dogs do not have a sense of right and wrong, moral justice, or conscience. Instead, they are self-interested creatures that learn what gets them rewards in life and what doesn't. Human values and moral standards can come into conflict with natural, normal dog behavior unless we teach them how to behave as a member of the family.

Dogs learn by trial and success: if a behavior is rewarded, they are likely to do it again. If it "fails" and they get no reward, they are less likely to try that behavior again. This works beautifully in your favor when you are trying to teach a puppy an obedience exercise, such as sit on command. If you wait for the pup to sit, and then give him a treat, the chances are that he will start to repeat the behavior over a period of time, in the hope of getting another treat. Equally, if you wanted him to come when called, and praised and petted him when he did so, you have increased the likelihood that he will return again.

However, few people consider the rewards that pups sometimes get from the enjoyment of the behavior, from the environment, or even from us—perhaps for behaviors that we don't want repeated!

intrinsic rewards

Some behaviors are self-rewarding to dogs. Actions such as digging, barking, chewing, chasing, and eating are natural canine behaviors and are repeated just because the dog has the opportunity. Prevention is the only solution for many of these behaviors—after all, it is impossible to cure a dog of being a dog!

environmental rewards

This type of reward is gained from a particular room or location. For example, a puppy invests some energy in climbing onto the dining room table when his owners have gone out. On top of the table, he finds some chicken and gobbles it up! Despite his owners' annoyance when they return, what do you think he will do the next time they go out? The puppy's behavior was instantly rewarded when he climbed onto the table and he will certainly try it again when he gets the opportunity.

accidental rewards from humans

Owners can sometimes accidentally reward their dogs for behavior that they don't like. For example, a puppy is

left Behaviors that are rewarded will be repeated!

sitting in the yard by himself. He is bored and a little lonely. He starts to dig a hole—just for fun. Suddenly, the backdoor bursts open! The pup's owner comes running into the yard, arms flailing and shouting at the top of their lungs. They rush toward the puppy and chase him away from the hole and around the yard, threatening to smack him.

To the puppy this is highly exciting. Not only has he been joined by a member of his family, but they are barking encouragement and seem to want to engage in a game of chase! This is much better than being bored and lonely—next time he feels this way, he is sure to dig a hole more quickly and see if he can make the fun start all over again!

Although this is an amusing scenario, many, many behavioral problems can start in this way. Even

above A trained dog is a safe, well-behaved dog.

serious aggression problems can sometimes be caused by owners believing that they are punishing the dog, when in fact they are accidentally rewarding it.

Think about your puppy and any behaviors he or she repeats on a regular basis. Perhaps he barks when you don't want him to, perhaps he chases his tail when visitors arrive, or steals food. Think about what rewards he gets for these and work on how to remove the reward, rather than attempting to punish your dog. In essence, intrinsic rewards can be moderated, environmental rewards removed from temptation, and accidental rewards depend upon the owner's attitude toward their pet's behavior.

communicating with dogs

left *Learning the basic rules of reward is a vital part of dog ownership.*

dogs don't speak english!

Of all the animals with which we share our lives, dogs are surely the most companionable. One of the main reasons for this is that we are able to communicate with them, understanding when they are happy or sad, depressed, or joyful, and can even anticipate their needs—all without the dog uttering a word! This remarkable relationship can sometimes lead owners to believe that their dogs understand what they are telling them. This, of course, is not the case—dogs cannot speak English, nor can they understand the meaning of words.

Instead, dogs are experts at making associations between words and actions—and are masters at watching and reading our body language and facial expressions. Over a period of time a dog can learn that the sound of a word such as "sit" means put your bottom on the floor. However, he could just as easily believe that "custard" meant the same thing! Equally, a dog may lower his head and put his ears back in anticipation of his owner's anger, if he has learned to associate the words "bad dog" with a punishment. This can lead the owner to believe that the dog "knows he's done wrong," when nothing could be further from the truth!

below *Even the youngest pup
can be trained to sit using simple,
gentle methods.*

reward and non-reward signals

Training a dog is like learning to speak
to a person from a foreign land. Both
parties need to take the time to learn a
little of each other's language and to
use body language and gestures that
they both understand. Shouting,
repeating the same words over and
over, and becoming frustrated do not
help! Instead, the clearer and calmer the
words and gestures are, the more the
other party will be able to understand.

Dogs thrive on clear messages, both
in learning basic obedience, such as
sit, down, and come when called, and
also in more general terms, such as
how they behave in the house.
Imagine how confusing it must be for
a dog to think that getting on the
furniture is allowed because one
member of the family encourages
him, and then being scolded for the
same actions by another. Equally,
being told to "sit" by one member of
the family may be no problem if the
dog has previously learned the word,
but being told to "sit down" by
someone else is meaningless.

your dog's dictionary

In order to save much time, energy,
and confusion, it is essential that you
create a doggie dictionary of all the
words that you are going to use in
training. Discuss these with your
family and come to an agreement
about what each training cue should
be and what you mean by them.
Attach the list to the fridge door and
make sure that everyone has read
them, then there is no excuse for using
different words for different actions,
and your pup's command of the
English language will be vastly
improved.

Your pup's name—look at me
Sit—put your bottom on the floor
Down—lie down on the floor
Come—come to me
Off—get off the furniture
Leave—don't touch

which puppy for me?

Choosing a puppy is not simple. It is vital that you are prepared to research and understand the kind of dog that it is right for you, and that you are ready to give the time, money, and commitment that owning a dog requires. In the modern world we struggle against the pressures of work, lack of free time, financial problems, and family dilemmas. Adding a dog into the mixture can make or break the situation—giving you a release and the chance to appreciate some non-judgmental companionship, or becoming just

another burden. If you have not yet made a final decision about getting a dog, or which dog to get, think hard and choose sensibly.

For many new owners, the type of dog that they choose is based on looks. Even if you decide to get a puppy from a rescue center, it is likely that the puppy's appearance will have a bearing on your choice. While it is important that you like the way your dog looks, it is vital not to judge the book by its cover. Plain puppies are often overlooked by prospective owners and yet they can have just as

much if not more to offer than their more attractive counterparts.

pedigree or crossbreed?

Pedigree dogs meet a breed standard. This means that you can accurately predict how large your dog will grow, have an idea of its overall appearance, and be able to make considered guesses at its behavioral characteristics. For example, it is easy to know that a black Labrador Retriever puppy will grow to about 22 inches in height at the withers, have a short, weather-proof coat, and

will remain black in color. It is also likely that the dog will have a predisposition to retrieving articles, enjoy swimming and water, and will probably like chewing as a youngster. However, it is also possible that a pedigree Labrador may have hip problems, eye defects, and arthritis in later years.

Crossbreeds—offspring of mixed or mongrel breeds—are more difficult to imagine as adults. Size, color, even ear-set can vary greatly and can change during development. It is also difficult to predict what kind of behavior such pups will display as adults, unless you can see clear indications of a historical past such as Collie or German Shepherd in their appearance.

However, crossbreeds and mongrels are generally less likely to suffer from hereditary problems, and have a reputation for being well-rounded individuals, if socialized and trained effectively.

left *Choosing a puppy isn't just about size and looks—temperaments vary, too.*

dog or bitch?

Much controversy surrounds this issue. Fans of male dogs will often claim that they are more affectionate and loyal than females, while devotees of bitches argue that they are less likely to show aggression and are generally calmer and more home-loving. Neutering can eliminate the hormonally linked problems in both sexes—hypersexuality and wander-lust in males and seasons in females. Whichever sex you choose, there is no substitute for ample socialization and training.

choosing a **pedigree** puppy

If you are trying to choose a pedigree puppy, have a look at the brief outline of the various groups below and then research your shortlist further by speaking to those people who already own and live with an adult of the breed. If you already have your puppy, take some time to check that you understand his/her historical and genetic background and find out what your pet was bred to do—it will enhance your understanding of their behavior enormously.

gun dogs

Gun dogs have always been very popular pets and, on the whole, have an extremely good reputation as family dogs. Many of the gun dog breeds retain strong working drives, and while this makes them easy to motivate in training, without sufficient stimulation they will find ways to amuse themselves!

The vast majority of retrievers and spaniels in this group love to carry objects around in their mouths and will happily pick up household items if a more appropriate toy is not available. This trait can lead to behavior problems if the puppy learns to be possessive over "forbidden" items, but is easily prevented by teaching the puppy to bring objects to the owner.

Many of the gun dog breeds, such as Labradors and spaniels, are also inclined to enjoy chewing as much as puppies—and this can lead to considerable destruction if an ample supply of chew toys is not supplied.

Most of the gun dogs appreciate free-running exercise and while it is important not to over-stretch the capabilities of young pups of any breed, from an early age it is important to teach them to come when called, especially as nearly all the breeds in this group love water!

hounds

On the whole, hounds are a strong-minded group. Bred to live and hunt in packs, they are usually strongly bonded to their owners and other family pets, but will think nothing of deserting them in favor of a scent in the park! Many of the hounds—particularly the larger breeds, such as Hamiltonstovare and Bloodhound—have a reputation as escape artists and can scale even high fencing if they are determined to get out of the yard to follow their noses!

left *A Golden Retriever puppy.*

above *Strong working instincts drive most hounds.*

right *Prewired for action—but the Boxer no longer has a job.*

The lower hounds, such as the Petit Basset Griffon Vendeen, Basset Hound, and Dachshund, may be smaller in height than their cousins in this group, but they retain an independent will that can often be described as stubbornness!

Substantial early training and socialization is required for all the dogs in this group, particularly if they are to be exercised outside off the leash.

working and pastoral

These two groups contain the herders and heelers—dogs that have been selectively bred to help man keep his flocks and herds together and to move them from field to field, as well as other working types, such as the Saint Bernard and Siberian Husky. The pastoral group contains many well-known favorites, such as the Border Collie, Briard, and Rough Collie.

The majority of all these dogs retain a great desire to herd moving animals, and without a flock of sheep this may well include your children, other dogs in the park, or—in a worst case scenario—joggers or cyclists. These are dogs that are more than capable of working for a full day and still have energy at the end of it—yet many are kept in conditions which rarely challenge their intelligence or activity levels.

Of all the groups of dog breeds, those in the pastoral group are the most likely to show inappropriate behavior in the home, primarily through lack of stimulation and adequate exercise. These dogs, and many of those in the working group, need a job to do, and while their original tasks may be impractical for a city dog to accomplish, they are adept at learning tricks, all types of training, and often excel at dog "sports," such as agility tests and flyball, a relay race where dogs negotiate an obstacle course and catch a launched ball. As puppies all members of this group need to learn to channel their chase instinct in an appropriate way through play with toys and extensive but enjoyable training.

terriers

Terriers were originally bred to chase rodents and other mammals, such as foxes and badgers. Some of these creatures can be quite formidable, particularly if trapped underground by a canine predator, hence these dogs needed to develop fast responses, courage, and a strong survival instinct. This means that many members of the terrier group can appear to be snappy, stubborn, and noisy—although they perceive the behavior as fun!

Many terriers are at the shorter end of the dog height range, so they can be mistaken for lap dogs—when nothing could be further from the truth! All the terriers need above-average amounts of socialization when young, particularly with other dogs. This is especially true of breeds originally intended for dog fighting, such as the Bull Terrier and Staffordshire Bull Terrier. Intelligent, fast, and reactive, terriers are loved all over the world by those who like their dogs to have real "personality," but are still prepared to put in time and effort to train, socialize, and be owned by a terrier!

toys

Toy dogs are the most at man's mercy. They have been selectively bred to be companion dogs, and thus many of them are small, if not tiny. However, it would be a mistake to assume that all toy dogs are lap dogs—many of them are more than keen to take as much exercise as you can offer and have large personalities in a small frame!

The Cavalier King Charles Spaniel is probably the most popular breed in this group, possessing an enthusiasm for life that is highly infectious and an outlook as hardy as a larger breed's, but in a conveniently compact package.

Many of the toy breeds are also highly trainable. The Pomeranian,

left *Terriers, like these Cairns, are usually outgoing and independent.*

above *Active, playful Dalmatians.*

left *A Cavalier King Charles Spaniel, bred mostly for companionship.*

Papillon, and ever-popular Yorkshire Terrier are all more than capable of being trained to a high level for many of the sports designed for "mini" dogs, such as agility and obedience.

utility

This group represents a rather ill-defined selection of breeds. On the whole, utility dogs have found themselves out of work, as the job that they were originally bred to do no longer exists. The Dalmatian is a good example. Bred to run behind horse-drawn carriages, this breed was most popular during the Regency period of the early 1800s!

Several spitz-type dogs belong in this group. The Akita, smaller Shiba Inu, and the Japanese and German Spitz all show the curled up-and-over tail carriage so typical of these types of dog, while their characteristics also retain some fairly basic instincts, such as hunting and protective behavior, which makes early training and socialization imperative.

where to find a litter

Having decided the breed that you want, your next task is to find a litter of puppies that have been bred and raised with the most care and consideration. Here, just one rule exists: buyer beware!

Unfortunately, few rules or laws currently exist which govern the breeding of dogs. Kennel Clubs in every country accept registrations from breeders who comply to their rules, but these may not always be to

the benefit of the puppies. This means that buying a pedigree puppy with Kennel Club registration is no guarantee of quality.

Kennel Clubs carry lists of breeders and this is a good place to start

looking. Bear in mind, however, that these breeders are not checked by the club that lists them, so you must personally inspect each litter until you find what you are looking for.

The puppies should be with their mother. This is because the mother's state of health and behavior gives a very good indication of how the puppies will behave later in life. The puppies should have been raised with their health and future behavior in mind. This means that they should not only have received the very best in food and veterinary care, but they should be well socialized and used to living in the heart of a family home. Ideally, the puppies need to have experienced all aspects of domestic life—they will have had a head start if they have been born and raised in a home, rather then in a kennel at the bottom of a yard.

Most conscientious breeders specialize in only one or two breeds. Be suspicious if several litters of varying types of puppies are available for viewing. Sadly, puppy farms are commonplace and recognizing them can be difficult.

breeder conditions and hereditary defects

The breeder should ask you many questions about your home and family life. Good breeders care about where their puppies will live and want them to have a happy life with the same household forever. Unscrupulous breeders are often more interested in how you are going to pay than how you are going to look after their pup.

Walk away if the conditions are dirty, the mother is aggressive, or if the breeder tries to persuade you to pay for and take a puppy there and then. It is far better to carefully consider your choice than regret a swift decision later. Be wary of buying a puppy from a pet shop or a dealer. Such puppies may have been separated from their mother too early.

Nearly all pedigree dogs require physical checks before they are mated, to ensure that they do not pass on unwanted hereditary defects. Hip dysplasia affects many of the large breeds; eye problems are also common.

Find out what defects exist in the breed(s) you like and ask the Kennel Club to tell you which checks the stud dog and bitch should have had before breeding. Ensure that you have sufficient information to interpret the results of any tests.

If you are not planning to show your puppy, you may find that a family home is an excellent source for a puppy. A pet bitch may not look like a champion, but if her temperament is sound, her physical checks are clear, and she has raised the pups in the heart of a household, her puppies are likely to be friendly and confident.

choosing a **healthy** puppy

On the whole, making sure your puppy is in the best of health before he or she leaves the mother is a matter of common sense. All the necessary physical checks require no scientific training. However, they do require that you follow your head, not your heart. It is not unheard of for puppies to spend the first week with their new owners at the veterinarian's, being treated for diseases or infestation by parasites that went untreated by the breeder.

Look at the litter as a whole. They should be bright-eyed and active. Of course, all puppies need to sleep a great deal, so if you arrive during a siesta you may need to return again an hour or so later to view them while they are awake. Once awake, they should be curious about you and want to play with each other and explore the environment. If one puppy has caught your eye, look at this one more closely and ensure that he or she seems to be healthy and free from parasites.

physical inspection

Eyes: should be bright and clear, with no discharge.

Ears: should be clean inside. The ear canal is hard to inspect, but it should be pink and clean, with no odor that might indicate infection or the presence of ear mites.

Mouth and nose: should be odor-free and cool. Some puppies have dark coloration inside the mouth and on the tongue; this is nothing to be concerned about and can even be a breed characteristic, as in the case of the Chow.

Skin and coat: The hair should be soft but resilient to the touch, the skin clear of dandruff or flea dirt. The latter is easy to detect as it looks like tiny specks of black dirt until it is made wet, when it becomes red as the dried blood dissolves. The coat should be in good condition all over. Bald patches around the eyes or muzzle can indicate the presence of parasitic infestation and should be investigated further.

Limbs: should appear to be straight and strong in most breeds and types.

Tail: Wagging and correct for the breed. A tail that is crooked or bent may indicate an untreated injury.

Abdomen: should be rounded, but not distended. Umbilical hernias are common in puppies and so the area around the navel and groin should be checked carefully for bumps under the skin.

Anal area: The area under the tail should be clean. Puppies can easily pick up infections that cause diarrhea and can be life-threatening.

Overall appearance: should be of a bright, healthy, and active puppy who is keen to explore and meet you. A puppy who seems lethargic, is sick, or has diarrhea, has discharge from any area of its body, or who scratches continuously may be unwell and should receive a veterinary check before it is brought home.

left *All pups need their sleep.*

right *A Bassett Hound puppy receiving a full health check.*

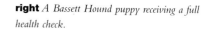

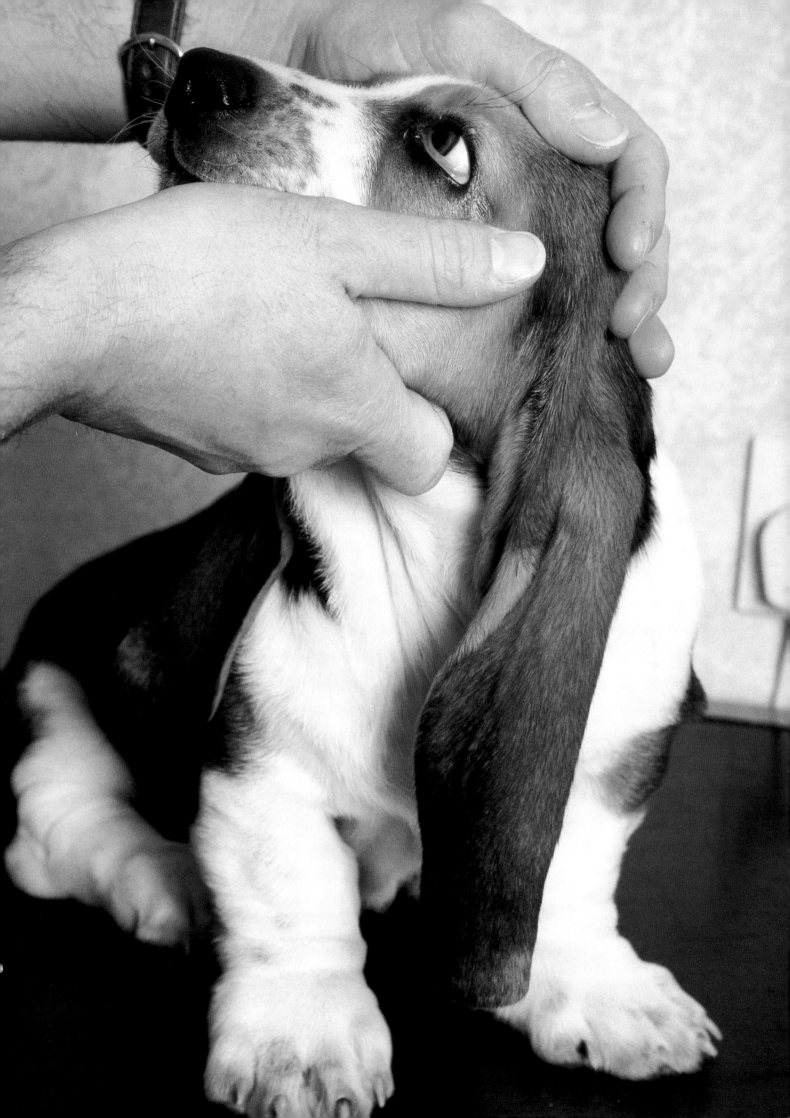

puppy behavior in the litter

Once you have determined the puppies' health, how do you choose one who is going to fit in well with your family? Some breeders and trainers use temperament testing at the age of seven weeks to determine the characteristics of individual puppies, but the results seem highly variable and depend heavily on the pup's state at the time and the individual carrying out the tests.

On the whole, the best choice for most families is the average puppy—one who is neither too shy nor too bold. This puppy is likely to be confident enough to cope with the busy routine of everyday life, and yet is not likely to be so bold that it tries to take over the household!

If the pups are awake, they should all be active and energetic. Eight-week-old puppies need a lot of rest, but on waking they need to urinate and then should get on with the serious business of playing and exploring. Any puppy who sits despondently at the back, refusing to come forward, is fearful of being held or handled, shies away from noise, or is defensive toward other puppies should be discounted immediately.

the small, shy puppy

The puppy sitting quietly in the nest may be deceptive. Although some shy dogs remain anxious all their lives, others develop strategies to get what they want without using physical strength. Pups like this can be very intelligent and "creative," making them ideal for owners who want to compete in some area of obedience or training, yet do not want an over-confident character. Certainly, this type of puppy is best for the experienced owner.

the average puppy

This pup may not be the first to climb onto your lap, but he will be keen to explore and to meet you. If you clap your hands, this puppy may move away if startled, but will quickly return to see what the noise was. If held carefully, he or she should not struggle too much, but will be happy to be petted and touched before being returned to play with his littermates. Here, he is most likely to play in equal amounts as the "aggressor" and the "victim."

the big, bold puppy

This puppy, too, may not be all he appears. Puppies who learn to use strength to achieve their aims may be confused when presented with a problem that needs a subtle solution! Given lots of socialization, these dogs are usually highly extrovert, confident characters. However, care must be taken to prevent this pup from bullying other dogs and may be best in the hands of strong characters who have experience rearing and training dogs.

Do not be downhearted if you are not given a free choice from all the pups in the litter. Breeders often keep a puppy for themselves, or they may have allocated particular puppies to show homes or for owners who wish to work their dogs in some way.

right *A bold puppy ambushes one of his littermates.*

Listen to the breeder's advice. Breeders often have many years of experience in selecting puppies to match prospective families. However, your puppy will be part of the family for the next 15 years, and it is important that you have a rapport with him or her from the start. Walk away rather than giving a home to a pup that you would not have otherwise considered.

below *Pups' confidence varies, even within a single litter.*

preparing the puppy's new home

If moving house is stressful for humans, imagine what it must be like for a puppy! Away from its mother and littermates for the first time, faced with strange sights, sounds, and smells, the majority of puppies feel a little daunted at first. This means that the more preparation you can do in advance, the more quickly your puppy will become settled in his new home.

safety first

The first and most important areas to consider are the pup's basic needs. As soon as you get your new puppy out of the car, the chances are he will need to relieve himself. You will probably want to take your puppy straight into the yard—and this is not the time to discover that there are holes in your fencing! A secure garden or yard is essential throughout a dog's life, but never more so than in those first weeks.

Once indoors, your puppy will probably want to explore. Puppies will sniff, chew, and lick almost anything, and that means that any

below *A box is a practical bed for a growing pup.*

potential hazards, such as electric cables, fragile ornaments, valuables, and toxic substances, such as cleaning solutions or medicines, should be well out of reach.

beds and bedding

Your puppy's bed should already be in place. Having decided what kind of bed and where to put it (see pages 84–85), make sure that it is cozy and welcoming—a soft blanket and an old soft toy give your puppy something to cuddle up to, but remember to remove any small

above *Ensure your yard is secure before allowing your new pet outside.*

plastic or glass parts that could be chewed or swallowed.

In an ideal world it is also very reassuring for a puppy to have an olfactory comforter, usually in the form of a towel or piece of blanket that comes home with him from the breeder's. This cloth will carry the scent of the puppy's dam (mother) and litter brothers and sisters and can offer comfort and reassurance at times when he might otherwise feel lonely.

dinner time

Dinner time comes around all too quickly and the essential message is to make sure that you give the same food as the breeder has been feeding for at least the first week. Puppies are prone to stomach upsets and a

change of food can create havoc with their digestive system and, subsequently, with house training. Make sure you have an adequate supply of the pup's usual food. Most responsible breeders will send you home with a small amount to ensure continuity, but check before you bring your puppy home.

the rest of the family

Make sure that your other pets are well prepared for the new arrival. Cats and older dogs can find their lives seriously disrupted by a newcomer. Cats particularly need a secure place of their own, preferably in a high place. This allows them to look down on the puppy and feel safe. Older dogs need to know that their position as number one dog is not being usurped, so ensure that the pup has a separate bed, feeding bowl, and toys.

---

pre-puppy check list
- Buy a supply of the same food as was given by the breeder
- Ensure you have separate water and feeding dishes
- Decide where the puppy will sleep. You can buy a dog bed, but a cardboard box with a warm blanket in a quiet area is fine at first
- Ensure your yard is securely fenced
- Phone your local veterinarian and find out when your puppy should have his vaccinations—and book an appointment
- Phone your local puppy class and ask if you can come to watch before you sign up
- Attend to any other pets. Cats may need a high hiding place, while rabbits and guinea pigs need secure penning
- Get a puppy collar and leash. This should be lightweight and comfortable—choke chains, prong collars, and other "correctional" collars should never be used on puppies

traveling with your puppy

For many puppies the first time they ever get into a car is on their journey home from the breeder's. Away from Mom and their littermates, this must be a frightening experience. Every aspect

below *A dog seat belt is a sensible precaution.*

that you can make less stressful will help to build positive experiences for the puppy for the rest of his or her life.

practicalities

Make sure that you have someone with you to help. It is impossible to drive and ensure that your puppy is

safe and comfortable, but with help, someone can sit in the back of the car with the puppy wrapped in a towel on their lap.

Bring some paper tissues, newspaper, and a plastic bag. Puppies are often sick on their first few journeys in a car and it is sensible to be prepared!

If you have an older dog who is friendly toward puppies, bring him or her along too. For many dogs, the best way to introduce them to the new pup is on neutral territory at the breeder's home, then allow the older dog to see that the pup is coming home with him in the car.

have a safe journey

On all subsequent journeys, make sure that your puppy is restrained in the car, for safety reasons. A restrained dog will be protected if you brake suddenly and cannot escape from the car when a door is open.

A crate is ideal, particularly if your dog will become accustomed to using one in the home. Make sure that it is placed somewhere stable. Dogs often feel less travel-sick if they cannot see out of the crate, so covering the top and sides can be reassuring. Alternatively, you can place your dog behind a dog guard that separates the back of the car from the passenger seats.

If your dog has to travel on a seat, use a special dog seat belt—a harness designed to clip into the seat belt holder and keep your dog in place. It is not advisable to allow a puppy to travel on the front passenger seat without restraint, or to allow him or her to hang their head out of the window as you travel. Eye injuries can easily result if debris flies into the eye at high speed.

the sounds of silence!

Start as you mean to go on and reward calm, quiet behavior in the car. Ignore

above *Dogs can find comfort and reassurance in a regularly used car crate.*

any squeaks, squeals, struggling, whines, or barks, even on that first journey. If the puppy learns on this occasion that he can make you join in with his noises by shouting or talking to him—or that he can win the jackpot and make you stop the car and get out to pet him—he may learn to repeat the behavior forever!

a word of warning

Dogs should never be left in a car on a hot day and should never, ever be placed in the trunk. Dogs quickly overheat and can die of heat stroke in a matter of minutes. Do not take the risk.

introducing other animals

First impressions count. As soon as your puppy steps through your front door, he or she will be learning about the new environment. If this first five minutes is crammed full of squealing children, the sniffs of an adult dog, and a cat's hissed warnings, the pup's impressions may not be favorable!

Try and bring your puppy home early in the day. This will give him or her time to settle down before having to be put to bed. It will also allow several brief and well-controlled introductions to other family members and pets that live in the household.

below *Introductions to "prey" animals need to be done early if attachments are to form.*

introduction to other dogs

Ideally, introductions to older dogs should be done on neutral territory. This may be best done in the yard, or even at the breeder's home, if you can take your existing dog when you collect your pup.

Keep your older dog on a leash, but allow him to sniff the puppy. On the whole, adult dogs are excellent with pups and are extremely gentle, but if you are unsure how your pet will react, be cautious on these first meetings. Once the initial greetings are over, lead your adult dog into the house first, allowing the pup to follow.

Give your older dog lots of praise and attention. He will need to know that he is still number one—and this will mean greeting him first, feeding him first, giving him affection, and playing with him first—even if this means ignoring the pup for a while.

Although this may seem hard, it is essential that your older dog does not feel the need to compete with the puppy, and both will be relieved that you are confirming and maintaining the pack structure that they instinctively understand.

Later on, you may need to reverse this process and favor the younger animal for "top dog" position. However, at this early stage, your puppy should be content to be lowest in the canine "pecking order."

introduction to cats

Cats are highly sensitive creatures that show their displeasure and stress in many different ways. It is essential that even dog-proof cats are allowed to come to know the new puppy in their own time, and that they have an escape route, should they want to use one.

During the first few meetings, make sure that your new pup is on a leash, so that you can prevent him or her from chasing the cat. Chasing is extremely

rewarding and it only takes one instance of chasing the cat out of the cat flap for a puppy to repeat the behavior forever. Ideally, give your puppy a chew or exciting toy to occupy him and encourage him to settle on the floor next to you, with the leash held loosely.

If your cat will come into the same room, make sure he or she has some tasty food to eat up on a high vantage

point, such as a windowsill. This will help your cat to feel secure and realize that with the puppy come good things. Several encounters like this will build most cats' confidence and will allow them to meet and mix with your pup more assertively over a period of time. Cats and dogs can be great friends if these first meetings are handled carefully.

right *It is best to introduce older dogs to the puppy on neutral ground.*

puppies and young children

It could be said that the only difference between puppies and young children is the number of legs! Puppies and kids can be bosom buddies or constant trouble, and require considerable amounts of adult supervision and training on both sides.

Puppies playing together bite each other, wrestle, and compete over resources. Unfortunately, until children reach about six or seven years old, it is all too easy for a puppy to treat a toddler as another canine playmate—with potentially serious consequences.

In order for any puppy and child to live happily together, basic ground rules need to be established and maintained. Puppies tire easily, and once fatigue sets in can become like petulant toddlers, irritable and even snappy. Interaction needs to be short and sweet, and it is essential that the puppy has a quiet place of his own to sleep where he will not be disturbed. Crates or indoor kennels are ideal for this purpose, as the puppy can rest safely inside, with a lock on the door to keep prying little fingers away.

below *Mirror image: young person and young dog.*

below *Mutual fascination!*
Puppies and children should
always be supervised.

To have a harmonious household, certain rules need to be applied:

● Children of all ages need to learn how to stroke and handle a puppy correctly, by tickling them on the chest and stomach, rather than bending over the top of the head, which may be perceived as a threat.

● Children should be told that putting their face or hair close to a puppy's face is an invitation for the puppy to play-bite them. While the puppy may not mean to cause harm, their sharp teeth can do considerable damage. Rough and tumble games can also lead to over-excitement and the risk of tears before bedtime. Hide and seek games with a toy, training games, and retrieving games are far safer and more appropriate.

● Children should not pick up a puppy. It is all too easy for a puppy to wriggle and fall, running the risk of injury, as well as negative associations with children that could last a lifetime.

children, training and health

Ideally, all children in the home should be involved with their puppy's care and training. Grooming, walking, and feeding all show the puppy that the human is in control, and give the puppy a reason to want to comply with their wishes.

Training needs to start early. Even a four-year-old child can be taught to ask a puppy to sit, lie down, and roll-over—a submissive posture for the animal to take—if the right kinds of gentle methods are employed. Puppies also need to learn how to take food gently from children's hands, while kids need to know that spare food should not be handed to the puppy during mealtimes!

Parents are often concerned about health risks associated with keeping a puppy in the home. Fortunately, these risks are almost non-existent, provided that sensible hygiene is practiced and that the puppy is kept free of parasites.

In order for your child to learn how to care for and train their puppy, the best possible instruction for both parties needs to be sought. Many puppy socialization classes welcome children, as long as they are supervised by an adult, and will help pup and child to learn together in a friendly environment.

sleeping facilities

It is essential that all puppies have a bed or area that they can call their own. In the first few weeks of life

below *Puppies gain comfort from soft blankets and cuddly toys.*

puppies need a lot of sleep and it is important that these periods are spent in a quiet place, away from family activity and safe from the attention of children.

Beds come in many shapes, sizes, and types, but the essential element to

consider is practicality. Puppies love to chew, so a bed needs to be durable, or cheap enough that its destruction will not matter. Comfort is important too, but not at the cost of hygiene—the dog's bed needs to be cleaned on a regular basis to ensure that flea eggs

above *Outdoor kennels are an option in temperate climates.*

Follow these points to ensure that your puppy enjoys rest and security in his crate:

● Introduce the crate carefully. Place a warm blanket and some toys inside to make it comfortable and enjoyable

● Leave the crate up and the door open so your puppy becomes familiar with it

● To encourage your pup to go inside, make up his dinner, put the dish inside the crate, and shut the door with the puppy on the outside! After a few seconds of trying to get to his dinner, open the door and allow your puppy to go inside. Leave the door open while he eats and allow him to come out whenever he wants

● If your puppy falls asleep during the day, gently pick him up and place him inside the crate, but leave the door open. To avoid accidents you must allow him outdoors to relieve himself as soon as he wakes

cannot colonize the area. Plastic and machine-washable fabrics are ideal—but avoid wicker, as it is tempting to chew and hard to clean.

To start with, a large cardboard box, with an old blanket or towels inside, may do just as well as an expensive bed, especially as it can be replaced if it becomes soiled or is outgrown.

crates or indoor kennels

More and more popular, particularly for puppies, are crates. These are indoor cages, with a door at the front or side that can be closed and even locked for security. If introduced in the right way, many dogs love these and regard them as total security and a home away from home if they are traveling in a car or are staying in an unfamiliar environment. They are also

an excellent aid to effective and "errorless" house training (see page 108). However, a cage is not to be used simply to keep the puppy out of the way for long periods of time.

Where you position the dog's bed or crate is usually one of practicality. However, while the bed should be somewhere peaceful, it is important that you can easily reach it, for cleaning and to move it occasionally. Some dogs become protective of their bed area if they feel threatened or if they are not used to people coming close to it, so a compromise needs to be reached.

nutrition: what to feed and how often

Recent research into the effects of diet has shown that it is not only the dog's health that can suffer if a diet is unbalanced or inappropriate, it can also have a significant impact on behavior, too. There are literally hundreds of different types of dog food to choose from, all with advertising campaigns to back up the manufacturer's claims. So how do you know which one to give your puppy?

types of food

There are two main types of ready-prepared dog food: complete, which means that nothing else need be added to the food, and complementary, which requires other constituents before it becomes nutritionally balanced.

The two types of food come in different forms, such as dried, semi-moist, and wet. Dried foods are usually found in sacks or bags and may need to have water added to them. Semi-moist foods are usually packaged in sealed plastic bags, while wet foods are usually tinned or contained in a plastic tube or roll.

However, whatever form of food you choose, the most important factor will be what's in it. Ingredients in dog food vary from good quality, easily digested materials, to poor quality, hard-to-digest fillers, which offer little in the way of nutrition to the dog, and simply keep the cost of the food low.

Dogs are omnivores in the wild, which means they eat both meat and vegetable materials. However, their teeth and digestive systems are designed for meat—the digestion of vegetable matter takes longer, uses more energy, and offers less nutritional value. This means that the most easily digested and usable sources of protein—vital for healthy growth, the repair of tissue, and for brain function and behavior—are chicken, lamb, turkey, fish, and eggs.

*Types of dog food—***above right** *canned,* **above left** *semi-moist, and* **right** *chicken added to biscuit.*

In view of this, which dog food you buy should be based on the list of ingredients, not the analysis on the side of the pack or the pictures on the front! At the top of the list should be a good quality source of pure protein. If the food contains "cereals" or "meat and animal derivatives," it is impossible to know what exactly is in the food and how digestible it is.

Unlike humans, dogs are content to eat similar food each day—indeed, they build healthy bacteria in the gut which helps to digest food, and this is reduced if the type of food is changed. For this reason, any change of diet usually needs to be done gradually, over a period of five to seven days, to enable the gut bacteria to recolonize and assist proper digestion.

above *Plastic, ceramic, and metal food and water bowls.*

eating up

Of course, any food needs to be palatable enough for a dog to want to eat it every day, and only your pet can tell you this! However, beware the games that puppies sometimes play. It is not unheard of for a puppy to suddenly decide that he is bored with one kind of food, no matter how good it is for him, and to persuade his owner to go shopping for a different kind. Then, after only a few meals, the puppy tries his luck to choose something different again. Eventually, such owners report that their dog will only eat human food—or worse, cat food, which is highly inappropriate for dogs—and that the

puppy would rather starve than eat anything else.

To avoid being "trained" in this way, ensure that your puppy has his meal somewhere calm and relatively quiet. Give him between five and 10 minutes to eat all of his food, then pick up the dish and keep it until the next mealtime if he has not finished the whole amount. Attempting to encourage a puppy to eat when it is full, stressed, over-tired, or distracted can lead to further problems later on and is best avoided.

diet and behavior

Sadly, many dogs live their entire lives on a diet that keeps them alive and relatively healthy, but does not maximize their fitness, or improve their behavior. Studies have shown that an optimum diet can influence a dog's

ability to learn new tasks, so it is all-important that you give the very best.

One way to judge your puppy's diet is to think carefully about his habits and health. Look at the list below. If your dog scores a "yes" to two or more of the signs below, you may need to consider a change of diet:

● **Lack of concentration** Your puppy wants to work hard for you in training and play but is distracted after only a few seconds, or becomes over-excited too quickly

● **Inconsistent digestion** Your puppy has minor bouts of diarrhea or constipation. They may need to go to the toilet more often than most—up to five or six times daily—and the feces may be large and smell particularly offensive

● **Chewing/eating unusual objects** particularly those which are fibrous, such as tissues, sticks, grass, soil, stones, coal, and even household items such as plastic, paper, and fabric

● **Eating large quantities of food,** yet remaining thin

● **Over-activity** even after exercise, and a tendency to perform a "wall-of-death" around the lounge furniture after eating!

● **Skin irritations** particularly itching at the base of the tail, feet, and belly. An increased tendency to suffer from allergic reactions to flea bites and pollen can also be linked to dietary factors

● **Bad breath or flatulence**

● **Coprophagia** the term given to the behavior of eating feces

Puppies use a lot of energy in growth and most need at least four meals a day at eight weeks of age. This can usually be reduced to three meals per day at 12 weeks and two meals per day at 16–18 weeks and older. However, bear in mind that every puppy has individual and variable requirements. Ask your veterinarian for advice if you are unsure.

below *Diet can affect behavior, as well as health.*

exercise

One of the main reasons why many people obtain a pet dog is to spend time with him or her, taking exercise together. It can come as a surprise to discover that your puppy may not be able to go out for that five-mile hike for quite some time! All puppies need exercise, and muscular development and mental stimulation depend on it. However, there is a risk of attempting to do too much too soon; as with so many areas of life, moderation is the key.

when?

As soon as your puppy is allowed to encounter the big, wide world, make sure that you get him or her out there! Most pups now finish their vaccination program at between 10 and 12 weeks of age, and at this time they should already be accustomed to wearing a light collar and leash.

where?

A short walk along a country road can be just as stimulating as a run in the park if your puppy is taking in all the sights, smells, and sounds along the way. Try to be imaginative about where you exercise your puppy. A walk along the high street can be a wonderful social experience, and offer a great deal in terms of learning and

training opportunities, while a run off-leash in a safe area away from traffic and other animals can be a chance to let off steam and simply be a dog!

how?

When you should let your puppy off the leash depends on a number of factors. If you have a clean, safe area of grass, such as a park or field where

left *Incorporate training into your walks through the park.*

90

dogs are allowed, your puppy has had all of his vaccinations and is relatively confident, then the earlier he comes off the leash and learns to follow you, the better!

Many people are worried about letting their puppy off the leash for the first time, thinking that he may run off and become lost. However, before the age of about four or five months, most puppies are relatively insecure outside and want to stick with their owner for security. This offers an ideal opportunity to reward your puppy for

coming when called and to give him a chance to socialize freely with other friendly dogs.

how much?

Up until the age of five or six months, puppies' bones are still forming and can be affected by too much exercise. Large amounts of jumping, galloping, and walking on hard surfaces can cause conformation problems later in life, particularly for heavy-boned breeds, but this doesn't mean a puppy should be over-protected. They need to let off

above *All dogs need the opportunity to run and jump freely.*

steam, build muscle, and enjoy social contact and training outside.

A puppy can tolerate short but frequent amounts of exercise, and an exhausted puppy tells you when he has done too much. Build up the amount of exercise that you give over a period of weeks, and by nine or 10 months of age, you will be able to walk, jog, and run with your dog as much as you like.

handling and stroking your puppy

picking up a puppy

No matter how large your puppy will eventually become, at the outset of your relationship you are likely to be able to pick him up and carry him. This allows handling skills to be practiced, and if carefully done can increase your pup's trust in you.

However, puppies can be incredibly wriggly, and one small mistake can result in dropping a pup. While this is unlikely to do the animal much physical damage, it may well cause him to become wary of human approaches, particularly of being restrained and handled. For this reason, it is important that children are not allowed to pick up puppies without strict adult supervision.

It is essential that the puppy feels secure and that its bodyweight is fully supported. Place one hand underneath the pup's chest, cradling this area and putting your fingers between his front legs. Your other hand should then scoop the puppy from underneath and support its bottom. The puppy can then be lifted onto a surface, your lap, or if you are carrying him, can be tucked well into the chest. Particular care needs to be taken when putting the puppy back down. Make sure

that you keep a firm hold until you can feel that the pup's bodyweight is back on the ground. Pups can sometimes try to jump when they are near the floor and this can cause an accident if you do not have a firm hold.

above *It is essential that children are taught how to handle puppies—gently and with respect.*

stroking your puppy

It may seem strange to learn that not all puppies like being stroked, cuddled, or handled! Indeed, many puppies have to learn that this kind of touch is pleasurable—they do not automatically find it rewarding.

To begin with, tickle the puppy on the chest area between his or her front legs. Watch the puppy closely. If he enjoys this, you can move on and stroke further up toward his face. If the puppy actively solicits more attention, move on and stroke his shoulders and sides. Leave his head and neck until last. Many dogs will offer you the part that they like to have touched—very often this is their rump or belly. Both of these areas are non-threatening and indicate that the dog is being friendly.

how to inspect your puppy

With your puppy standing, look into each eye. Encourage him to look at a toy or tidbit if you need to distract him.

Move onto your dog's ears. Lift the ear flap away from the head and look right down the ear canal. Praise your dog for calm behavior.

Now lift your pup's lips, first one side, then the other, to allow both sides of the teeth to be seen. Then open the mouth very gently to look at the tongue and throat. Be confident and gentle. Praise and give a special treat for good behavior.

Next, move on to the neck and shoulders. Feel every inch of his skin and coat, moving gently down the front of each leg. Lift the front feet in turn to look at your puppy's nails, then tuck the foot under, to inspect the pads. Gently probe between each toe.

Moving back up to the shoulders, run your hands down the flow of the coat to the hips, and then down to your pup's ribs. Feel down each hind leg, then inside the thighs. Lift both rear feet in turn and inspect them as you did the front ones.

Finally, stroke down the whole of your puppy's body, from the head to the tip of his tail. Hold his tail up firmly at the base, to allow you to look at this anal area. Then slip your other hand underneath to check the belly and the genital area.

Be generous with praise and tidbits during the whole procedure. Your pup should soon learn that being examined in this way is pleasurable.

grooming

Many owners automatically imagine that only long-coated breeds need substantial amounts of grooming. However, even the smoothest-coated dog needs to have his or her ears cleaned, teeth brushed, toenails clipped, and coat bathed from time to time. In view of this, all puppies need to be handled on a daily basis (see pages 92–93) to ensure that they are confident and happy about being touched and groomed all over. Practice plus reward and praise for calm acceptance and not chewing the brush or other tools will stand you in good stead for the rest of the dog's life.

above *An array of brushes and combs are available for different tasks, types of coat, and means of use.*

brushing

All dogs should learn to enjoy being brushed. The type of brush eventually used will depend on the length and nature of the dog's coat, but in puppyhood the essential part of the exercise is that it is pleasurable. For this reason, choose a soft gentle brush—rubber ones are ideal, as they tend to massage the skin rather than pull through the hair. If using a brush with any kind of pins, try it on your own head before using it on the puppy to find out how little pressure you must use. With your puppy standing, hold a treat to distract your pup and use your other hand to brush all over his body. Give praise all the

left *Choosing the correct brush makes it easier for the puppy to become accustomed to grooming.*

time for good behavior. After a few sessions you should be able to brush him without having to rely on using the treat as a lure, but continue to give one afterward as a reward for good behavior.

combing

Use the comb for feathering and fine hair around the face and ears. Be particularly careful that you do not pull or tug at any knots beneath the surface. It is better to cut these out than cause a negative association with the comb in the early days.

trimming

The amount and type of trimming that your dog will need depends on its breed and whether you intend to show your pup. If so, follow your

breeder's advice and start little and often, giving rewards for good behavior and making the whole experience a pleasurable one.

If you intend to have your dog professionally trimmed or stripped (where dead hair is removed by hand) by a groomer, try to find one on recommendation and ask them specifically how they handle puppies. Do not think that professional grooming is a substitute for practice at home, however—it is even more important that your puppy is used to being handled in this way if he is to be groomed by a stranger later on.

ear cleaning

A pup's ears should be inspected regularly by lifting the ear flap and wiping the flap and visible parts with a

above *Cleaning a dog's ears is easy—if he doesn't struggle!*

soft tissue, or dampened cotton ball, if necessary. Never use any kind of tool, such as a cotton bud, to push down the ear canal. This is a highly sensitive area and could cause damage to the dog's ear drum and hearing. Seek veterinary advice immediately if you find a brown discharge or if the ear canal smells offensive, as ear infections are common and usually require treatment.

eyes
In some breeds or individuals, the eyes weep a little and leave a brown discharge that stains the coat underneath. Regular wiping of the tear patches with a dampened cotton ball is recommended, but don't use ointments, drops, or other substances unless prescribed by a veterinarian.

teeth and mouth
Just like us, dogs benefit greatly from regular dental care. Cleaning a dog's teeth is not as difficult as it might sound if this procedure is started early on. Specially designed dog toothpaste is available that has the right chemical formula to suit dogs—and it has the bonus of tasting like chicken or liver!

Put a little paste on one finger or a finger brush and apply by rubbing gently on the teeth and gums, working from front to back, sweeping the brush from the gum down the tooth, to dislodge food particles and to gently massage the gums. Ideally this should be done at least once a week.

feet
Some dogs require the hair trimmed from between their foot pads and nearly all dogs need their toenails clipped every three to four months, depending on the surfaces on which they are exercised. A great deal of patience is needed to teach the puppy to accept this procedure calmly and quietly—many dogs loathe the experience!

It is essential that only the tip of the nail should be removed, as the blood supply to the nail—the quick—runs the length of the nail and ends quite close to the surface. If accidentally cut, this can be very painful and will bleed profusely. Many owners have so much trouble clipping their pet's claws that they take the dog to the veterinarian to have it done. This is acceptable if you are concerned about the task, but bear in mind that this gives extra stress to most dogs and can build negative associations with both the veterinarian and having their feet handled.

bathing

Most dogs only need bathing about twice a year, if they are groomed regularly and are not prone to rolling in offensive-smelling dirt! Bathing too frequently strips the coat of natural oils and waterproofing.

Baths should be given as calmly as possible to avoid stress or over-excitement. Shampoo, a positive attitude, and lots of towels are required! Make sure that the water is warm, but not hot, and that you rinse all shampoo out of the coat thoroughly. Dry and brush your pup afterward and keep him warm—it is easy for damp dogs to become chilled if care is not taken.

clipping your puppy's nails

1. Leave the clippers in the cupboard! Train your puppy to accept having his feet handled, one at a time. Offer him a food treat and pick up each foot in turn, then give the treat. Repeat this several times a day for at least three days.

2. Pick up each foot in turn and this time hold it firmly, while extending one claw so that you can inspect it for at least five seconds. Do this for each claw on each foot, giving the puppy a food treat for calm behavior. Repeat this frequently over three or four days.

3. Now get the clippers out, but do not try to cut any claws. Show the puppy the clippers and give him a treat. Do this several times until he really looks forward to seeing those clippers!

4. Hold each foot in turn and extend a claw. Tap the clippers on the claw lightly, then give the dog a treat. Do not cut the claw. Do this for each nail on each foot and repeat it until your puppy is calm and confident with the procedure.

5. You are now ready to cut the claws, but you need to ensure that you do not cut the quick. Cut no more than 1/25 in off the end of each nail. You can always cut more off later, but you cannot undo the damage of severing the quick. Give a "jackpot" reward for good behavior of several treats and a good game.

6. Cut your dog's claws little and often. Frequently clipping the nails encourages the quick to recede from the end of the nail, making an accident less likely.

left *If you cannot use a toothbrush on your dog, rubbing a dental hygiene pad helps keep the mouth clean.*

70g

hygiene and the law

Owning a dog carries great responsibilities, both in the home and in public areas. Sadly, dogs are now banned from public areas in many countries—and in some cities in Russia and Iceland they are banned from being kept as pets!

below *Good early socialization prevents problems when your pup meets different animals.*

clearing up

Much anti-dog feeling is created by one single issue: dog excrement. Allowing your dog to foul in a street, public area, or anywhere where children may have contact with it, is irresponsible and potentially hazardous to health, but is easily avoided by simply clearing up after your dog wherever you go. Poop scoops are readily available from pet shops and

even some supermarkets, but an ordinary plastic bag will do just as well.

Dogs, particularly puppies and pregnant bitches, also need to be treated regularly to ensure that they are free from worms. This is particularly important, as the egg of one specific canine parasite, *toxacara canis*, can cause eye defects if swallowed.

Health risks from dogs are minimal if basic hygiene precautions are

followed, such as washing your hands after handling a dog and before eating. However, this tiny risk can be minimized if your dog is regularly wormed. This should be done on the advice of your veterinarian at three- to six-month intervals and is as simple as giving a tablet.

Fecal sampling and testing can be done for owners who are concerned about giving unnecessary medication on a regular basis. This allows the veterinarian to see whether parasites are present in the feces, and to dose with wormer medication if necessary.

good manners

All dogs can cause problems in public if they do not behave in a suitable manner. Early socialization with people, other dogs, and habituation to traffic, other animals, and the hustle and bustle of urban life can prevent the vast majority of problems, and combined with training, ensures that you have a dog who is welcomed by the community, rather than resented.

Attacks by dogs on members of the public are relatively rare, but road accidents caused by lost or straying animals are far more common and can have fatal results. It is absolutely essential that yards and homes are made secure so that dogs cannot escape and cause a nuisance in the street or countryside.

Even if you have spent a great deal of time and effort in training your dog, do not assume that it is reliable in every situation. Puppies have short attention spans and can be listening to their owner one minute and chasing

above *Always clean up after your dog with a poop scoop.*

leaves in the wind the next! Always make sure that off-leash exercise is done in a safe area and keep your puppy on the leash anywhere where traffic or livestock may be present—it could save his life.

don't lose out!

In most countries, it is a legal requirement for dogs to be marked with some form of identification— either by means of a collar and tag or a more permanent identification mark, such as a tattoo in the ear or inner thigh, or a microchip (see page 100). Check your local by-laws to find out what is required in your area.

identification

There are two main methods of permanent identification available to dog owners. Both are intended to be used in addition to a collar and tag, but in the event that the collar is lost or removed, the owner can still be easily traced.

identichip

Identichip is the name given to the insertion of a tiny microchip under the dog's skin. This carries information about the dog in the form of a unique serial number that can then be fed into a computer to trace the owner's details.

right *Some form of visible identification is a legal requirement in most countries.*

The microchip is about the size as a grain of rice and is inserted using a hollow needle. The needle is usually placed between the shoulder blades and the chip injected in the same way as an ordinary vaccination. Some puppies find this uncomfortable and may squeal or wriggle, while others barely seem to notice the procedure. In order to read the information stored on the chip, a scanner is placed directly over the area of skin where the chip is inserted until a read-out is obtained.

Microchipping has been a controversial method of permanent identification in some countries, as instances of chips migrating around the body

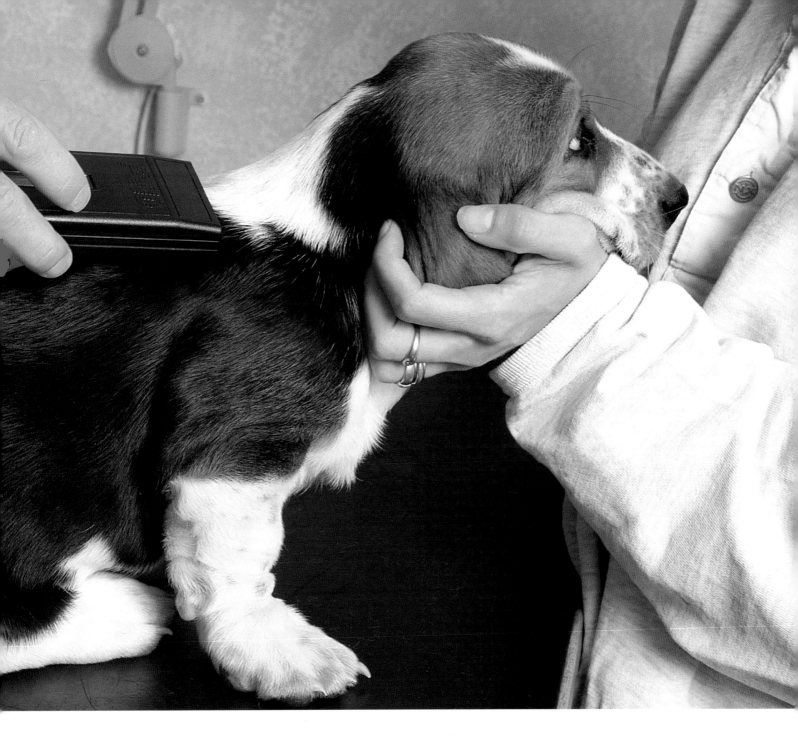

have been known. While this is unlikely to present a health risk, the scanner may not detect the chip if it is far from the usual insertion point and the lost dog's identity will remain unknown.

tattooing

Tattooing is the other common method of permanent identification for domestic dogs. This is usually carried out when the puppies are only a few weeks old. Just like human tattoos, the marks are made by injecting tiny amounts of ink under the skin, usually to form a unique identification number that is listed on a computer. Unlike human body art, however, these tattoos are applied

using a small tool that imprints the whole number at one time, causing brief, minimal discomfort. Once again, some sensitive puppies may cry out when this happens, while others do not react at all.

genetic fingerprinting

The most recent advance in identification comes to us straight from the science lab. New methods allow dogs to be identified by their DNA structure. This is analyzed by taking a small swab of saliva from the dog's mouth, which is examined in the laboratory. The dog's individual genetic make-up is logged onto a computer, and later matched with records, should the pet be lost.

above *This Basset is having his newly inserted microchip scanned.*

In these days of worldwide travel there is no reason why our pets should be forced to stay at home. However, permanent identification will become a mandatory issue if we are to protect them from disease and loss. Even closer to home, it is essential that your dog is able to be reunited with you if the unthinkable happens and he goes missing. If your puppy does not already carry one of these forms of identification, talk to your veterinarian or local pet rescue center to discuss the options.

choosing a veterinarian

You need to select the very best in private health care for your puppy, but unless you have had a dog before, choosing a veterinarian can be difficult. The best way of finding a good veterinarian is to act on recommendation. Before you get your puppy, ask other dog owners in the area which veterinarian they use and what services are available. Your pup's first visits to the vet are likely to be for vaccinations and a bad experience can put your puppy off veterinarians for life.

large or small

Veterinary practices range from the small and cozy to the large and expansive. Small practices often provide familiarity—you are likely to be seen by the same veterinarian each time and build a history with him or her. On the other hand, large veterinary hospitals have more technical equipment and expertise. Some veterinary hospitals not only operate and hospitalize animals on site, they even have their own laboratory testing services.

Puppy parties have become increasingly common among many veterinary practices in recent years. These are an excellent opportunity to

right *Your veterinarian is not only there to treat emergencies, but to prevent illness, too.*

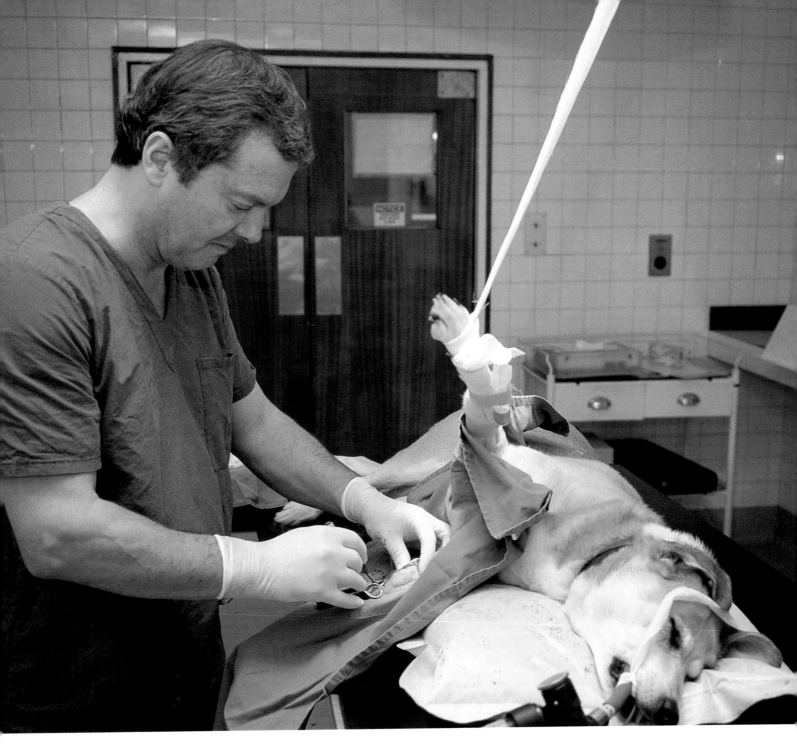

take your pup along to the vet before he is 12 weeks old to familiarize him with the environment, the nurses, and the handling procedures that will be necessary later in life. This exercise helps to convince your pup that the veterinarian's office is a friendly place—not simply where needles are stuck in the back of his neck.

opening hours and procedures

Once you have located a suitable practice, make sure you ask about procedures and opening times. Larger practices have veterinarians on-call 24 hours a day, while others share an "on-call vet" over evenings and weekends.

Make sure that office hours will suit your daily routine, and that the staff are friendly and helpful. Imagine how you would feel if your puppy was ill and needed overnight care. Are the staff caring and the facilities suitable? Would you feel comfortable leaving your puppy in their care?

Ask too about vaccination requirements and routines. Some veterinary practices offer early vaccination, which allows your puppy to begin socialization early. Others use homeopathic nosodes, rather than chemical vaccination, or may prefer to give a bi-annual booster injection rather than a yearly jab. A good

above *Operating facilities vary from practice to practice and may influence your choice of veterinarian.*

veterinary practice will be happy to spend time talking to you and helping you to choose the best options for your puppy.

Registering your puppy with a veterinarian as soon as possible is a sensible strategy. This will mean that your details will be available when you first take your puppy in, that way you can concentrate on introducing him to the staff and making new friends in this new environment.

a **safe** environment

At eight weeks old, your new puppy is approximately the developmental equivalent of a three- or four-year-old human. Just as most children of this age need constant supervision to keep them safe, young puppies need protection from the potentially damaging results of exploring their new surroundings.

Unless carefully taught otherwise, all dogs divide our environment into four simple categories: things to eat, things to chew, things to chase, and things to use as a toilet. If left to their own devices in our homes or yards, puppies will perform perfectly normal dog behaviors, which, from our perspective, are often highly inappropriate. Inadequate supervision inevitably results in habits which are, at best, irritating and expensive, involving the replacement of your own or others' property, and at worst, life-threatening and expensive, in the form of veterinary bills.

For example, it is generally safe for your pup to chase a ball in your yard; doing the same with a cat across a busy road is not advisable. Doggy treats are tasty and safe; other edible items are potentially lethal. A puppy left alone in the yard may chose to occupy himself with the chew-toy you have left him, but your azaleas, gravel path, or compost heap may be more inviting. For a new

left *Caring for a puppy is a fine balance between freedom and safety.*

puppy, learning when, where, and what is safe requires our intimate involvement and informed guidance.

playpens

As no one can supervise a puppy 100% of the time, many of the same safety devices that we use for babies and young children can be considered. The use of stair gates, fridge and cupboard locks, as well as puppy playpens and indoor kennels, provide safety when our attention is elsewhere.

play safely

Suitably sized and non-destructible toys, which cannot be swallowed whole or chewed into swallowable pieces, are essential for all pups.

Although a traditional dog occupation, chasing sticks is highly dangerous and can cause serious injury to the mouth and throat. Safe and edible chew-toys, such as large hide chews, are normally safer than bones, which can splinter. Cooked chicken bones are particularly dangerous.

Do not leave your puppy alone with squeaky toys—not only will they not remain squeaky for long, but the "squeak" may end up in the puppy's stomach and potentially cause an intestinal obstruction. Other commonly swallowed items include babies' pacifiers, socks, marbles, and toys from cereal packets—indeed, anything left lying around the house will be seen as a potential chew-toy by your puppy. If

for no other reason than to keep him safe, the arrival of a new puppy should herald an unprecedented degree of tidiness from the whole family!

Many dogs learn to swallow an item in order to "hide" it, particularly if someone else seems to want it! Don't run the risk of endorsing this dangerous habit by chasing the puppy—teach him to drop the item instead by offering a tasty food treat in exchange.

Supervise your puppy closely when he is playing with other animals or children. Although an expertly timed scratch on the nose may teach him that the family cat should be approached with respect, a similar injury but to the surface of the eye may have far worse consequences.

choosing a kennel

For most people who keep a dog, there is one major drawback—they are a tie. What happens when you want to go on holiday and need to leave your dog behind? A number of options are available and it is always wise to consider which option would be ideal before you book your dream cruise.

boarding kennels
Boarding kennels are usually designed to take a number of dogs at any one time and care for them on-site. This has the advantage that your dog is cared for by experienced individuals, has a chance to get exercise, and is likely to have plenty of other dogs to look at during the day! However, it is not unheard of for dogs to come home thinner and hoarse from barking after a stay in kennels if they are unused to the experience, and it is highly stressful for some.

how to choose a kennel
Try to find out about kennels in your area on recommendation from other dog owners. Make sure that you inspect the kennels before booking in your puppy. The standard of kennel accommodation varies greatly from luxury apartments with doggie duvets, heat lamps, and even furniture in each den, to the most basic with newspaper on the floor and a wooden bench to lie on. Check that the kennels are clean and that all fencing is safe and secure.

However, perhaps more important than the accommodation is the attitude and experience of the managers and staff. Always ask to see where your puppy will be housed

during his stay. Will there be sufficient stimulation for him? What exercise regime is offered? Are the staff knowledgeable and caring? What contact with people will your dog have while he is there?

Good kennels know that puppies need comfort and play in order to enjoy the experience of being away from home. Many will keep puppies away from the noise of barking from the main block and house them next to smaller or older dogs where an extra eye can be kept on them.

It is worth finding a good kennel early on if you intend to use one regularly during your dog's life—it will be so much easier if he or she gets used to the routine as a puppy than suddenly being expected to deal with it later on.

home sitters

For those who prefer not to put their dog in kennels, a useful alternative is a homesitting service. Prices vary, but at least you have the comfort of knowing that your dog is in its own home, with a caring and knowledgeable person looking after it. You can also be assured that your plants will be watered and your lawn mowed while you are away!

Register with a reputable company or agency for this service. Dogs can learn a lot of bad habits in a few days if they have a poor sitter.

leaving your dog with friends

The best option is to leave your precious pup with someone you know and trust. This can work extremely well, as long as some basic rules are set before departure. Tell your friends what your puppy likes and dislikes, as well as

what he or she is permitted to do at home. This helps to prevent disputes between friends on your return when you discover that your puppy now likes to sleep on the sofa and drinks from the toilet bowl.

Prepare a list of useful numbers for your friend before leaving. Include your veterinarian's telephone number and your pup's insurance details and make sure they know what to do should your puppy become ill while you are away. Looking after someone else's pet is a great responsibility and it is reassuring to have an emergency plan already formulated.

house manners

house training

Developmentally, young puppies are just like babies and cannot be expected to have total control over their bodily functions—particularly at night—until they are between eight and 10 weeks old. However, by using an approach called "errorless learning," puppies quickly learn what is expected and do their utmost to relieve themselves in the right place, rather than in the home.

Errorless learning means never allowing your puppy to make a mistake by going to the toilet in the wrong place. Learn to predict when your puppy will need to go to the toilet—after playing, after waking up, after any kind of excitement, such as the children coming home from school, and straight after meals.

At these times, take your puppy to the same place outside and wait with him, even in the rain. Gently repeating a word or short phrase, such as "be quick," helps your puppy remember what he's there for. As soon as your puppy starts to sniff around or circle, praise him very gently. Once he has relieved himself,

lavish him with praise and give him a really special treat as a reward.

In between these events it is wise to take your puppy outside about once an hour, just in case he should need to go. Watch him closely for signs that he might need to go, such as sniffing or circling.

crates and mistakes

If you wait outside with your puppy and he does not go to the toilet, bring him back inside. He is likely to need to go in the next hour so supervise

right *Accidents are sure to happen, so make sure you have odor eliminator, disinfectant, bucket, cloth, gloves, and scrubbing brush.*

above These house-trained Sable Border Collie pups are toileting at the same time!

him constantly. If you cannot supervise him during that time, you need to put him in a crate or playpen, or in an enclosed area where you do not mind if he has an accident. The advantage of confining your puppy for very short periods when you cannot supervise him is that most dogs do not want to soil their sleeping area, and will therefore try to wait until you take them out again.

If you catch your puppy in the act of going to the toilet, or about to go, at any another time, say "outside" in an urgent voice, then take him quickly outside to show him where you do want him to go, even if it's too late to save your carpet! If he gets even one drop in the right place, praise your puppy.

Being cross with your puppy for making a mistake in the home is pointless. Dogs soon associate any mess with your anger, not with the act of going, and simply show fear when you find it, or worse, learn to eat their own excrement. It takes years for a child to be fully toilet trained, but no one would consider punishing a baby for having an accident in an inappropriate place. Old-fashioned punishments, such as rubbing the dog's nose in its own mess, are abhorrent and counter-productive and should never be used.

Many people use sheets of newspaper to teach their puppy to go to the toilet where they want them to, but compared with the "errorless" approach it is harder work in the long term, as you need to housetrain your puppy twice—once to paper, and then again outdoors.

greeting behaviors

One of the most important things a puppy can learn is how to greet people properly. Dogs greet each other by sniffing each other's mouths, then sniffing rear ends, and finally, by jumping and playing—hardly appropriate when saying hello to humans, but perfectly natural to a dog!

To teach a new puppy that humans need to be treated differently to canine friends, it is vital that kind, gentle ways are used. Gone are the days when it was thought acceptable to smack dogs or knee them in the chest if they jumped up—such punishment can teach once-friendly dogs to be wary and suspicious of human beings.

right *Sniffing the rump is normal canine greeting behavior.*

The vast majority of puppies who have not yet learned good bite inhibition (see page 58) try to mouth people when they are excited, which can be painful and frightening—especially for children. While this behavior is normal, it needs to be controlled if it is not to become a habit.

Three effective ways to teach your puppy how to greet humans:

● **Sit:** This is probably the easiest method for most people—and it has benefits for the puppy too, as nobody can resist stroking a puppy who is so well-behaved. First, it is necessary to teach the pup to sit on cue (see page 114). Once this has been accomplished, you will need some volunteers to help you practice the next stage. They should walk toward the puppy, but ignore him until the owner has encouraged the pup to sit. Once the puppy is sitting, the visitor can greet and stroke him. If the puppy jumps up at any time, the visitor should immediately fold their arms and turn away, to reject the behavior. As soon as the owner has encouraged the pup to sit again, they can resume petting. This method takes consistency, but is very clear for the pup to understand.

● **Ignore rowdy behavior; praise and reward good behavior:** This method requires the puppy to be on an ordinary collar and leash when the visitor arrives. The visitor should completely ignore the pup, no matter what he does to get their attention, and continue a conversation with the owner regardless. Most puppies try pulling, barking, jumping, and leaping to get to the person, but soon give up when they realize it is pointless. The owner can then gently praise the dog for being calm. This method is particularly useful for puppies who are very demanding, since it teaches them that they are not always the center of attention.

left *Jumping up is a common but inappropriate greeting behavior. Train your puppy to sit instead.*

● **Carry a toy:** Many dogs, particularly gun dog breeds, love to hold a toy or article in their mouths when greeting people, and this often seems to stop them jumping up. If your puppy is one of these, keep a special toy by the front door. Do not allow your pup to play with this toy at any other time, otherwise it will lose its novelty. As soon as your visitor arrives, hand them the toy to give to the puppy. This also prevents young puppies from mouthing visitors, especially children, while they are still going through the play-biting stage.

clicker training and teaching attention

Clicker training is one of the most modern and scientifically based training methods. It is also fun for you and your puppy! Clicker training means that you do not have to push, pull, or otherwise force your puppy to do anything—indeed, hands only touch the puppy to bring rewards and praise, rather than coercion.

what is a clicker?

A clicker is a small plastic box that contains a tiny sheet of flexible steel. When pressed, this sheet makes a distinctive "click, click" sound. Over a very short period of time your puppy can learn to associate this sound with getting food, toys, and praise—rewards for good behavior. This sound then "marks" the good behavior that earned the reward, much like putting a check-mark on a page next to a correct sum at school!

timing skills

Using the clicker makes the timing of rewards much easier for both dog and handler to understand. It clearly indicates to the dog why he got the reward and means that he can be creative and use his brain to discover what achieves the sound and what doesn't.

Dogs who become "clicker-wise" can perform amazing training feats. Many of the assistance dog organizations, which train dogs to help their disabled owners by putting lights on and off, operating elevator buttons, and bringing in deliveries, are training using clicker principles.

If you do not have a clicker, don't worry. All of the principles of clicker training can be used simply by substituting the sound of the clicker

above *The clicker, for signals of reward, and training discs, for signals of non-reward. Both tools give dogs clear information.*

for a unique sound that you make with your voice. You can use a word, such as "yes," or "right," or simply make a double-click sound in your mouth.

To begin with, your puppy is sure to make mistakes. However, mistakes do not represent failure, only feedback. If you ask your pup to sit and he refuses, he is not being naughty, but is lacking in motivation or simply does not understand you. Ignore his mistakes—do not click or treat—and he will soon work out that only the responses you are looking for bring him rewards.

why use food or toys?

Sadly, some owners still believe that a dog should do what they tell it because it "loves" them. This is like us going to work each day for the love of the company! Dogs need to learn that praise is rewarding, and while it can be a powerful tool, the vast majority of pups need more of a "salary" to motivate them to go to work. Find out what your pup likes best, usually small pieces of tasty food or a favorite toy.

basic clicker training

Make sure you and your puppy are somewhere calm and quiet, such as your den or the yard. Have some

right *This dog is taking a treat in response to an ambiguous hand signal. Clickers can clarify the command-action-reward process.*

really tasty, small treats, such as cheese, sausage, or chicken, at the ready. Hold the clicker behind your back at first—there is no need to point it at your puppy, and you should avoid clicking too near his ears.

● Say your puppy's name in a happy voice
● As soon as he looks at you, click and give a reward
● Repeat this three or four times.
● Soon, your puppy will understand the meaning of the clicker and react to the sound, thinking, "Great, where's my treat?!"

You will also have taught your puppy to pay attention when you say his name. Now you are ready to move on to other exercises and tasks.

sit, down and stay

teaching your pup to sit on command

● Keep quiet and show your puppy you have a food treat in your hand. Put it on his nose, right up close.

right This puppy is being taught the "down" command.

Now lift your hand up and back, so he has to look right up to follow your fingers. The movement of him looking upward causes his rear end to go down

● Suddenly your puppy is sitting! As soon as his bottom hits the ground, click, or use your clicker word, then give your pup the treat

● Repeat this a few times (if your puppy's front legs come off the ground, your hand is probably too high)

● Now you can say the word "sit" just before you move the food lure. In a matter of minutes you have taught your puppy a verbal request to sit, plus an effective hand signal. Congratulations!

● Next you need to phase out the food lure. With no food in your hand, ask your puppy to sit. If he does so, click immediately and give a food treat. If your pup does not sit when asked, help him with the hand signal, then reward for good efforts

below *With use of command and treat, the "down" movement is achieved.*

● Practice until your puppy's sit movements are quick and totally reliable by asking him to sit before he gets anything he likes—having his dinner, having his leash put on, being let out into the yard. It's his way of saying "please" and "thank you"

teaching your pup to lie down
The "down" needs a little more patience than the "sit," because you have to wait for the puppy to do the right thing. Keep watching your pup and be ready for that moment of genius!

● With the food lure on the puppy's nose, lower your hand down to the floor, directly between the puppy's front paws. Hang onto the treat by turning your palm down, with the food hidden inside your hand. This way, the pup will want to burrow his nose underneath, and will turn his head sideways to nibble at it

● Indications of imminent success are: the puppy raising a paw to try and get the treat from your hand, the front end going down in a play-bow position, and moving backward slightly. All these

things mean you just have to wait. Eventually the back end flops down to the floor, too

● The instant your puppy lies down, click or give your clicker word, then drop the treat onto the floor and let the dog eat it. (This prevents the puppy following your hand back up again like a yo-yo!)

● Repeat this several times, sometimes with the food in your hand, sometimes without. Once you can guarantee that your puppy will lie down by following your hand to the floor, you can add the word "down"

removing the lure
● Stand up straight. Quietly ask your puppy to lie "down," but this time don't help him with a hand signal. Most dogs will try sitting, or even giving a paw, before having the idea that lying down might work. Be patient and try not to repeat the cue word

● The instant that your puppy lies down, click or give your clicker word, then give a jackpot reward—several tasty treats and a game!

● Repeat this several times in several

different places in the house and yard until your puppy responds reliably anywhere and everywhere

stay
Once your puppy has learned to sit or lie down on command reliably, you can teach him to stay in that position for longer, by waiting before you click and treat.

● Ask your puppy to sit or down, count to five, then click or give your clicker word, and treat

● Ask your dog to sit or down, then count to ten and click, then treat

● Ask your dog to sit or down, then count to two, and click and treat

● Ask your dog to sit or down, count to 30, then click and jackpot treat

Make sure that you keep your puppy in position for random amounts of time, and build up to about two minutes. Praise all the time he is sitting or lying down. The click ends the behavior, so make sure that you click while the pup is still sitting or lying down, then treat two or three seconds later.

returning when called and leash walking

teaching your pup to return when called

Your puppy already knows that when you say his name, he needs to look at you. If this needs some revision, now's the time!

● Stand directly in front of your puppy, say his name and waggle the food lure in your outstretched hand. If he moves toward you, click or give your clicker word, and immediately give a treat

below *Call your puppy to you from mild distractions, then build up to more involving ones.*

● Repeat this, but now move backward one or two paces and encourage him to come to you for clicks, praise, and treats
● Increase the distance your puppy has to come to get the food—sometimes only one step, on other occasions 10–12 paces
● When your puppy comes to you reliably, add a word—"come" or "here"—after his name

You are now ready to add another element—as soon as your dog reaches you, touch his collar, click or give your clicker word, and give him the treat. This teaches the dog to come to you and wait while you hold him before

he gets his reward. Practice these exercises by calling your dog for a click and jackpot of treats, his dinner, or a game, when he least expects it:

● Call your dog to you from another room
● Call your dog in from the yard
● Call your dog when you are sitting down
● Call your dog away from distractions, such as birds in the yard

If your puppy is very slow or doesn't come when called, do not be tempted to punish or scold him—this will only make him more reluctant next time!

Instead, show him what he could have earned and then put the food or toy away. Go back to basics and teach him to pay attention to his name if necessary.

teaching your puppy to walk on a loose leash

The main reason why so many dogs pull on the leash is that they get rewarded for it! Dogs perceive that by pulling they get to the park more quickly and can lead their owner to where they want to go, rather than the other way around. Dogs need to learn when they are behaving nicely on the leash, and this is where the clicker really comes into its own. Rather than scolding the puppy for

pulling, non-reward it by simply standing still. When the pup is in the right place, let him know by clicking and treating.

● Put your puppy on the leash in the den, hallway, or yard. Stand still to begin with
● As soon as your puppy puts slack in the leash and looks at you, click and treat, then start walking in any direction you choose
● Watch your puppy's position carefully. If there is tension in the leash, stand still. Do not move off again until the leash is slack
● Every time there is a loop of slack in the leash, click and treat
● Repeat this a few times, then stop and have a game
● Now, tuck the food into a pocket. Click the correct position, then produce the treat. Be generous with

the food to begin with, then gradually reward only the best responses
Once your puppy behaves reliably on the leash, you can begin to practice outside on walks. Don't expect too much too soon! You may stand still more than you walk forward to begin with, but be patient. On days when you are in a hurry, use a head-collar to prevent pulling from becoming a habit. Head-collars, such as the Halti, fit the muzzle and allow kind, precise control. Click and treat when your puppy is in the right place while wearing the head-collar to hasten your training.

Using this method, all dogs can be taught to walk nicely on an ordinary flat collar and leash or head-collar and leash. Choke chains, prong collars, and other so-called "correctional" devices are totally unnecessary and can easily cause injury.

leave and retrieve

teaching your puppy to leave objects and food alone

"Leave" or "off" is probably the most vital command you can give your puppy in the early weeks! Puppies are like toddlers and seem to want to explore the world by picking things up with their mouths to check how they taste and feel. A reliable "leave" command makes the puppy remove his nose and mouth from the item—or even better, he doesn't touch it in the

first place. This means that food being eaten by others is safe from pilfering, cats and other animals can walk past your puppy without being pestered, and unpleasant substances in the park can be avoided!

teaching the "leave" command

● Make sure you are somewhere calm and quiet. Hold a treat in your hand and close your fingers tightly around it
● Present your hand to the pup and wait while he sniffs, licks, and nibbles, trying to get the food. Do not say anything
● Watch carefully. As soon as your puppy takes his nose away from your hand, even for a split second, click or use your clicker word, then give the treat
● Repeat this several times

● Now repeat the exercise, but this time wait until the pup has taken his nose away from your hand for the count of two, then click and treat
● Build up the amount of time that your pup will wait with his nose well

left The "leave" command can be particularly useful during the holidays!

away from your hand to about 10 seconds. At this point you can add in the cue word—"leave" or "off"—in a calm, quiet voice, not a threatening one
● Once your puppy has got the knack, repeat the exercise, but this time say "off" or "leave," then present the food on your open hand. If the puppy tries to take it, simply close your fingers around the food—do not jerk your hand away

Over a period of repetitions, most puppies rapidly learn that the word "off" or "leave" means that they must not touch—and this can be extended to objects on the floor, outside, and so on.

teaching your puppy to retrieve on command

The art of teaching your puppy to retrieve lies not in teaching him to run out and pick things up, but to teach him to hold objects and give them to you.

● Start with a toy or object that your puppy likes. This can be a rag, cardboard tube, or dog toy. Have some tasty treats ready

above Some breeds retrieve naturally; others need training and practice.

● Holding the object in your hand, offer it for the pup to sniff. If he even touches it, click or use your clicker word, then treat
● Repeat this a few times, then wait for something a little more. This time you are looking for the pup to try and take the object in his mouth. If he does, let him hold it for one second, then click and treat
● Build up the time he will hold the object to about 20 seconds, then click and treat. When he starts to be reliable, add the cue word "hold" just before he takes it

Next you can put the object on your knee, or on the floor and ask him to hold. Once you have mastered this, no matter where the object is, your puppy will understand that "hold" means go and pick it up, and bring it back for a click and treat. Usually, playing with toys like this is so self-rewarding that the clicks and treats can be rapidly phased out, then the pup will play retrieve games just for the fun of it.

protecting your puppy

right *The sooner your pup is vaccinated, the sooner he can go out into the wide world.*

vaccination

Certain routine and preventive procedures are essential to ensure that your puppy remains as healthy as possible throughout his life. These are part of responsible dog ownership. Vaccination against the four major infectious diseases of dogs—canine distemper, hepatitis, leptospirosis, and parvovirus—has been very effective in reducing these illnesses to their current low incidence.

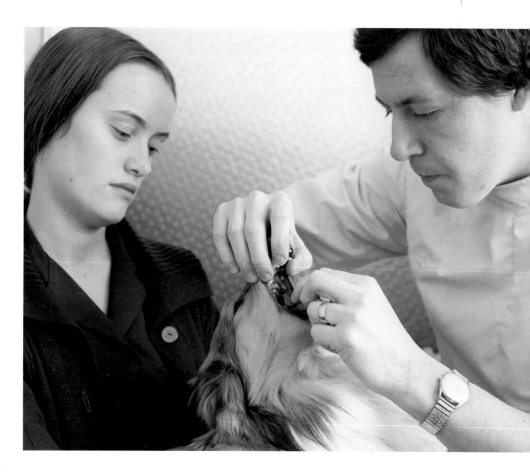

Occasionally, someone will confidently declare that their dog lived to a ripe old age without immunization, so why bother with their new puppy? Such lucky dogs, however, have merely benefited from the actions of the very many conscientious owners whose vaccinated pets have given disease organisms nowhere to breed, thus reducing the overall risks for all dogs.

Canine distemper, hepatitis, and parvovirus are viral conditions, and as such cannot be treated with antibiotics once contracted. Whether a puppy survives or not depends entirely on its level of immunity, hence the importance of vaccination.

A new-born puppy is initially protected by antibodies generated in the mother's body and supplied in the first few days of milk. For vaccination to be effective it must be administered at the time when maternally derived antibodies are falling to low levels in the puppy's bloodstream. The generally advised ages for first and second vaccinations are at eight and 12 weeks respectively. However, some vaccines have recently been found to be effective at 10 weeks of age, thus allowing earlier exposure to the outside world and socialization with other dogs.

A puppy can be allowed to mix with other adult dogs before he or she has finished the vaccination course, as long as you know these dogs are up-to-date with their own vaccinations. As entering a new home and the first vaccination are the biggest stresses a young puppy will be subjected to, lessen their effect by allowing the puppy a few days to acclimatize with you before his first vaccination is given. Similarly, if a first vaccination has been given by the breeder, wait a few days before taking the puppy home.

parasites

The most common puppy worm infection (the round worm, *Toxacara canis*) is picked up before birth by larvae crossing the placenta, or after birth via the mother's milk, or by eating eggs passed out in the mother's feces. Puppies should be wormed regularly from the age of four weeks and should therefore be free of any significant worm burden by the time they reach their new home, particularly if their mother was wormed during pregnancy.

If any adult worms remain, however, eggs passed out in the puppy's feces may be ingested and cause reinfection. Migration of the larvae through the body, particularly the lungs, causes damage and poor growth, as will the presence of adult worms in the intestines. In addition, there is the very small risk of infection of humans,

particularly children, by contact with wormy puppies.

The tape worm, *Dipylidium caninum*, has the flea as its intermediate host. This means that rigorous flea control, as well as

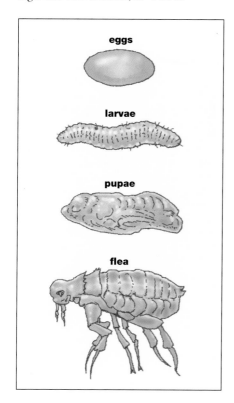

eggs

larvae

pupae

flea

left *Cat fleas are as common on dogs as they are on cats!*

is very important to treat the infestation as soon as possible. The adult fleas carried on the puppy will quickly begin laying eggs in the warm and dry environment of a home; within as short a period as 12 days, the eggs can develop into adults also capable of breeding.

There are a number of preparations available to combat flea infestation, but the most reliable and effective are supplied only by prescription by your veterinarian. Insecticides come in the form of powders, sprays, and liquid "spot-on" preparations. The latter are applied in small quantities directly

worming, is required. Any new puppy should be given four doses of an effective multi-worming medication at two-weekly intervals and thereafter two to three times per year to prevent damage to themselves and any risk to humans.

The ubiquitous flea, most commonly *Ctenocephalides felis*, shared by dogs and cats, is the cause of much distress to both dog and owner. At any one time, approximately 5 percent of fleas are present on the dog, with 95 percent living in the animal's environment. The presence of fleas on the skin can cause constant scratching and chewing and it is not uncommon for advice to be sought, not for the dog's sake, but because he is keeping his owners awake at night!

If a dog becomes allergic to the saliva of the flea, scabby and infected lesions may develop all over the body but particularly along the back and the back of the thighs. In a small puppy, a heavy infestation of fleas can cause clinical anemia and associated weakness, as the fleas feed on the puppy's blood.

If you suspect your puppy has fleas, it

right *Vaccinations can be traumatic but are essential for your pet's health.*

onto the puppy's skin and are the most effective, in terms of the drugs used and ease of application. In addition to treating your pup, the home should be treated with a suitable long-acting insecticidal spray and thorough vacuuming.

Multi-animal households may require an additional approach to flea control, with a non-insecticidal method given in the form of a monthly tablet. This effectively prevents the fleas from breeding.

neutering

One of the most important preventive health care discussions you can have with your veterinarian is about the advantages and timing of neutering your puppy. Although most people agree that both sexes are more content when free of their sex drive, there is still some debate among veterinarians as to the best time in the puppy's development for these operations. Addressing this topic early enough allows you to make an informed decision about your individual pet and find out how early your veterinarian favors neutering.

The castration of dogs affects those behaviors driven by the hormone testosterone, but will not, as is often assumed, "calm him down." Male dogs can be neutered from 12 weeks onward, but this is not necessarily advisable. On the whole, dogs need to mature before being castrated, and the ideal time seems to be between eight months and a year. Conditions such as testicular cancer and prostate disease are generally prevented if neutering is done before middle age.

Spaying (ovariohysterectomy) of the female prevents ovarian tumors and pyometra, a serious womb infection very common in older unspayed bitches. There is considerable evidence that, in addition to these benefits, spaying a bitch at six months of age—before she has had her first season—substantially reduces the risk of her developing mammary cancer later in life.

Urinary incontinence may be seen in bitches spayed at any age, but seems to be more prevalent in those who are allowed to become overweight. It is often assumed that putting on weight is a foregone conclusion following spaying and castration, but sensible dietary management and lots of exercise prevents obesity and its associated health risks.

below *Dogs are anethetised before undergoing operations.*

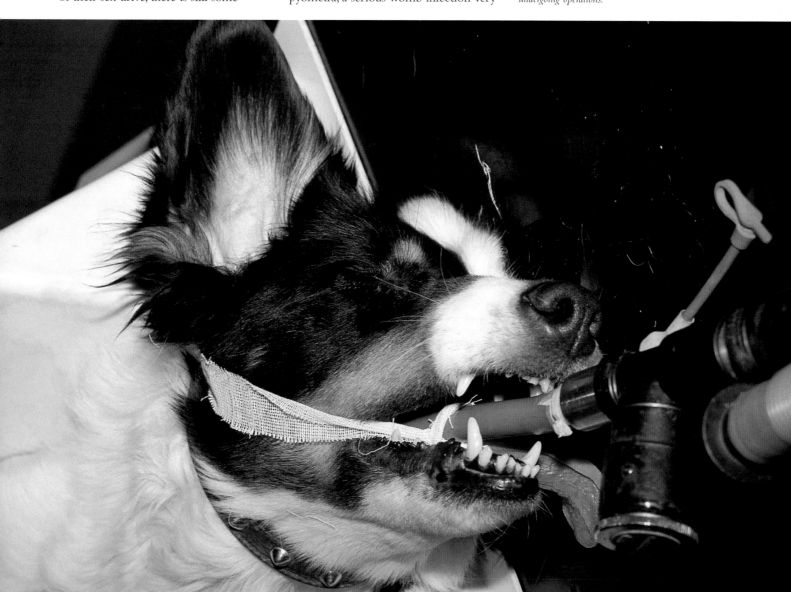

common puppy health problems

All common health problems in puppies can be divided into two categories: those that may have come with the puppy on purchase, which may be congenital or disease problems, and those that become evident later on, which may be developmental problems, injuries, or caused by organic disease.

below *Adult teeth can grow misaligned and cause gum irritation.*

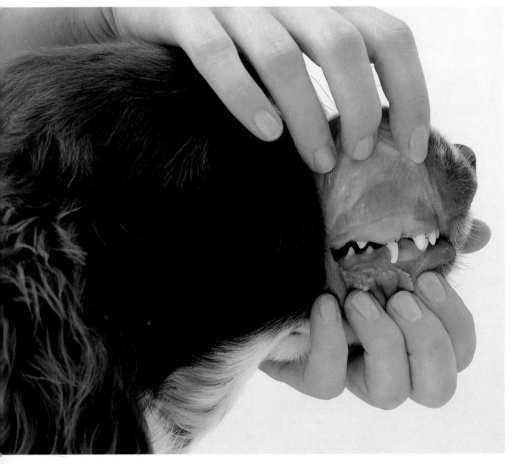

common problems present at purchase

congenital problems

Congenital problems are those which are present at birth and may be caused by genes that the puppy inherits, by spontaneous genetic mutation, or may have developed within the womb. They include certain breed-related conditions, some of which may be evident at a puppy's first check-up by a veterinarian.

Congenital defects in puppies include entropion, whereby the eyelids roll onto the surface of the eye, cataract, a defect of the lens of the eye which may result in glaucoma and blindness, and patella luxation, a displacement of the kneecap resulting in varying degrees of lameness. Such conditions may require surgery and will therefore have welfare implications if you are not prepared for this possibility.

Your veterinarian may be alerted to a heart defect by the presence of a heart murmur, detectable with a stethoscope. Although in some instances heart murmurs may be of no clinical importance, they are often associated with poor growth, low exercise tolerance, and short life expectancy. Some heart defects can be surgically corrected by a relevant specialist.

Inguinal or, more commonly, umbilical, hernias are frequently seen in young puppies. Although easy to spot, unsuspecting owners are sometimes told that these defects will "go away on their own." Sadly, they do not, and it is important that affected dogs are not bred from later, as they are likely to pass on the defect to their offspring. Surgery is required to correct hernias, which can be carried out at the same time as neutering if there is no immediate risk to the puppy.

Conformational defects, such as undershot jaw (inferior prognathism), where the lower jaw extends below

above *Extreme thirst can indicate an underlying problem, such as kidney disease.*

below *Many ailments can be controlled with a course of pills.*

the upper, may be considered desirable in brachycephalic (short-nosed) breeds, such as the Boxer and Pekingese, but can cause discomfort in other breeds or crosses, where the teeth hit the gums in the wrong places. As this can be painful and interfere with chewing, dental realignment or extractions may be necessary once the adult teeth have grown in.

diseases

Disease problems evident at purchase include external and internal parasites, such as fleas, lice, and worms, and are seen all too commonly at first vaccination, as is the black, crumbly ear wax associated with the presence of ear mites (*Otodectes*). As with flea infestation, scratching and irritation is caused but is usually confined to the area of the head and neck.

These infestations are all preventable by appropriate routine treatment of the mother and other animals they come into contact with. Their presence suggests that the puppy's background and care has been less than ideal.

Certain breeds, such as the Staffordshire Bull Terrier, are prone to carrying the demodectic mange mite, which lives in hair follicles. It typically does not cause irritation, unless associated with infection, but causes hair loss and baldness, sometimes with flaky, dry skin. Demodectic mange mites are not contagious.

The sarcoptic mange mite, on the other hand, causes intense irritation, scabs, and hair loss and is contagious to other dogs, as well as causing lesions in affected humans.

common problems later in life

developmental problems

Developmental problems are usually breed- or size-associated and are less likely to be clinically evident after a young dog reaches maturity and growth ceases. Intermittent lameness that shifts from leg to leg, typically in adolescent German Shepherd Dogs, suggests panosteitis, an inflammation within the cavity of long bones that can also lead to excess bone formation.

Problems arising from the growth plate (epiphysis), the area of soft, uncalcified bone where growth occurs, can result in an unattached portion of bone, such as in "ununited aconeus" in the elbow, mainly in German Shepherds, or premature closure of the plate, resulting in distortion of the forelimbs and associated pain and lameness.

Insufficient blood supply to the developing hip joint, particularly in small breeds such as the Yorkshire Terrier, can result in Legge-Perthes disease, causing crumbling of the head of the femur. This condition usually requires surgery to alleviate the associated pain.

Hip dysplasia is caused by a laxity, or looseness, of the ligaments holding the head of the thigh bone in position. This excess movement leads to abnormal wear on the joint, deformity of the articular surfaces, arthritis, and often considerable pain. Although, surprisingly, some dogs do not show symptoms until osteoarthritis develops later in life, suspicious signs of a swaying gait and weak hindquarters are seen in typically affected breeds, such as the Labrador and German Shepherd, as early as five or six months of age.

Craniomandibular osteopathy is an extremely painful condition resulting in excess growth of bone on the lower jaw and its articulation with the skull. It is seen in small dogs, such as the West Highland White Terrier—hence the term "Westie jaw"—and Cairn Terriers.

right *A skin scrape is being taken to learn if mites are present.*

Retained deciduous teeth (milk teeth) are common in toy breeds and occur when the root of the baby tooth does not dissolve away as it should. If still present by the age of eight to nine months, it is likely that they will need to be extracted to prevent distortion and damage to the newly erupted adult teeth.

injuries

Despite all our best preventive measures, traumatic conditions and accidental injuries can occur in all ages of dog, but certain types are seen more often in puppies and adolescent dogs. Toes and tails being trodden on or shut in doors can result in fractures or dislocations. The softer bone of young dogs is less likely to shatter on impact than in the mature animal; they tend to bend and crack lengthwise instead, causing "greenstick" fractures, which are usually harder to detect without X-ray photography than breaks suffered by older dogs.

organic disease

The most common symptom of disease seen in puppies is diarrhea, with or without vomiting. Both are reactions of the gut to the ingestion of potentially harmful substances—essential in naturally scavenging animals.

Most cases of diarrhea are caused by the puppy eating something he is not accustomed to, whether a new brand of dog food or part of yesterday's takeout. If your puppy seems bright and lively and still willing to eat, he should be starved completely for at least 24 hours after diarrhea is first seen, followed by two to three days of a light and easily digested diet, such as chicken and rice or pasta. However, if your puppy seems listless or depressed, if he is also vomiting, or if blood is noticed in the diarrhea or vomit, your veterinarian should be contacted for advice without delay. It may be that your pup is running a temperature and that some kind of infection is involved.

above *This veterinarian is checking the injured dog's heart function.*

You are likely to be asked to take the puppy to the vet for examination and treatment.

Occasionally, a puppy who has been suffering from diarrhea suddenly becomes very listless, stops eating, and ceases to pass anything at all. This may be indicative of an intussusception, where part of the bowel folds in on itself and causes complete obstruction. Veterinary help must be sought immediately.

Juvenile pyoderma is the canine equivalent of acne and is caused by bacterial infection of the hair follicles. It is commonly seen on the muzzles of short-coated young dogs, such as Rottweilers and Dobermans, and may result in permanent scarring if not promptly treated with a long course of antibiotics.

accidents and emergencies

right *A thorough examination is required after any traffic accident, even if no injury is visible.*

If you suddenly become concerned about your puppy and are unsure whether the problem constitutes a real emergency, it is always safer to telephone your veterinarian for advice in the first instance. Even if your call is out of routine business hours, most reasonable veterinarians would prefer to be disturbed unnecessarily and be able to give reassuring advice on the phone, rather than run the risk of missing a potentially serious case.

road traffic accidents

Any puppy involved in a road traffic accident, however minor, should be checked by your veterinarian as soon as possible. Animals have a misleading ability to run away from the scene of an accident, in spite of serious injuries, and internal bleeding is not always immediately evident.

If the puppy does not appear able to move or has been knocked unconscious, lift him onto a blanket, which can be used as a stretcher, and cover him with another to maintain body heat. Do not be unduly concerned about moving such a patient—the quickest way to get veterinary treatment is to take the dog directly to an animal hospital or vet's office, preceded by a telephone call to say you are on your way, rather than to wait for help to arrive. At the hospital, a puppy can be given intravenous fluids and medication to counteract shock and be kept under observation before decisions about radiography and surgery are made.

injury from attack

Very occasionally, puppies are badly injured in attacks by larger or older dogs, particularly if they have been bitten on the chest or abdomen. Urgent treatment must be obtained, and again, hospitalization may be necessary to stabilize the puppy and fully assess the damage. Small skin tears and puncture wounds should receive attention within 24 hours, since fight wounds are very likely to become infected and require antibiotic medication.

accidental injury

Injuries to dogs' ears or foot pads may bleed alarmingly, even when the wound is very small. As a first aid measure, apply firm pressure with a generous wad of cotton batting and bandage before taking the puppy to the vet. Ears should be bandaged close to the head to prevent flapping and further bleeding. Do not feed the puppy or allow him to drink in case stitching under general anesthesia is required.

If your puppy becomes suddenly lame and cries out in pain during play, it is worth remaining calm and waiting half an hour before rushing to the vet. Many of these episodes seem to be the canine equivalent of a struck "funny bone" and the puppy quickly returns to normal with no ill-effects. However, should the lameness and pain continue, telephone for advice.

poisoning

If you suspect your puppy has very recently swallowed a potentially harmful substance, such as drugs intended for people (birth control pills are a "favorite"), the induction of vomiting is recommended. This can be

carried out by dosing the puppy with a strong salt solution or crystals of washing soda.

Warfarin-type rat poisons, which cause death by preventing blood clotting, are rarely harmful in a single incident, unless large quantities are swallowed at once. This type of poisoning is more commonly seen among farm puppies and dogs with continued access to poisoned bait.

above *Wrap an injured dog in a blanket, to maintain its body heat.*

Urgent veterinary attention and administration of the antidote is required, as by the time symptoms of weakness and breathlessness are noticed, the puppy may be severely anemic.

common behavioral and training problems

introduction

It would be wonderful if all puppies came into this world knowing just how to behave around humans and other dogs. Dogs are not machines, however, and they can often behave in ways that are challenging, difficult, or even exasperating—a puppy who isn't sometimes naughty would be unique!

Throughout all the many challenges that any owner will have with their puppy, the important factor is to try to

right Dogs are not small, furry humans! Try to "think dog" when trying to solve problems.

below A well-trained and behaved pet is a loved and valued part of the family.

"think dog!" Try thinking about the situation from your puppy's point of view, not just your own. Imagine why your puppy is behaving as he is. What rewards is he getting from the behavior and how you can remove them and reward different, more acceptable, behavior instead?

On the whole, nearly all behavioral and training problems are normal actions for the dog. Dogs bark, dig, urinate and defecate where they see fit, play rough games, chew, jump up, growl, and even bite as a normal part of their repertoire—it's only because humans find these behaviors inappropriate or unacceptable that they are problems.

Of course, prevention is always better than cure. Extensive early socialization, training, and habituation give the puppy

a head-start in understanding human ways so that he is less likely to put a paw wrong later. However, socialization is often inadequate, training inappropriate or missing, and habituation distinctly lacking—all through no fault of the owner. Equally, all these areas may have been covered extensively, and yet your puppy has decided to break the rules and be a little monster anyway, despite all your work!

Throughout any kind of rehabilitation or retraining, it is essential that the human part of the equation is calm, aware, and understanding. Punishment is nearly always counterproductive and can lead to further or longer-term problems, and even the break down of the relationship between dog and owner.

There is little point in embarking on a program to alter a puppy's behavior if you feel tired, angry, or upset. Your puppy will only pick up on your frustration and start to mirror your

emotions. Instead, plan your retraining program away from the crisis. Sit down with a cup of coffee, paper and pen, and write down your goal for the end of the training program. This needs to be couched in positive terms, with a target of what you want your puppy to do in place of behavior you don't like—rather than what you want him or her to stop doing! For example, "I want Fido to sit when he greets people," rather than "I don't want Fido to jump up." Once you know where you are headed, the journey is easy!

barking
Why do puppies do this?
Dogs and puppies bark for a number of different reasons: to raise the alarm about intruders, to call the rest of their "pack," to show distress or fear, and as a display of aggression to keep away animals or people that they feel threatened by. Many dogs also bark in sheer excitement.

below *Barking is natural, but is often a nuisance in urban areas.*

Why is it a problem?

Apart from aggression or defensive behavior, the majority of dogs bark for attention or to try and call their owners when they have been left alone. This can cause disturbance for neighbors, annoyance for owners, and may even be dangerous if it distracts the driver when the puppy is in a car.

Solution

Prevention is certainly better than cure for this one! Many owners inadvertently encourage their puppy to bark by laughing or praising when he first barks at the door or when outside.

If barking is already a problem, ask yourself why your puppy may be doing this. If he is barking at other dogs, is there fear involved or is it sheer excitement? More socialization and training will be required.

If your puppy barks at you for attention, make sure you non-reward the behavior by getting up and leaving the room, turning your back on your puppy, or putting him in another room for a few minutes. Giving eye contact, shouting, or telling your puppy off are all likely to make matters worse—he may think you are joining in! Teaching your puppy to bark and "shush" on command can work well. (See pages 112–119 for more help with teaching new tasks.)

jumping up
Why do puppies do this?

Dogs jump up to be friendly! As young puppies, dogs learn to greet each other by licking and nuzzling at the mouth and lips of their mother. Later this becomes a greeting gesture that is used among dogs. In order to reach our faces, dogs have to jump up!

Why is it a problem?

Jumping up may be okay if you are wearing old clothes and are fit enough to withstand the physical

pressure involved. However, jumping up is often inappropriate, as it may harm small children, the elderly, or the frail, and is considered "bad manners" by most people— even if they love dogs! Muddy paws only add to the annoyance this behavior can cause.

Solution

As jumping up is usually friendly behavior, particularly in puppies, it is totally inappropriate to use any kind of aversive technique to prevent it. Instead, think about what you would prefer your puppy to do when greeting people—either keeping all four feet on the ground, or even better, sitting.

Teaching "sit to greet" is relatively simple. First, make sure that all jumping up of any kind is ignored. Turn your back and fold your arms if the puppy jumps up; praise and pet if he is sitting or being calm.

Next, ask a friend to stop by your home; have your puppy ready on a leash. When your friend arrives, they should ignore your pup completely. Both of you must ignore the pup when he attempts to gain attention by jumping up.

When your puppy tires of jumping up and instead tries sitting or lying down, click or give your clicker word, praise, and give a food treat. Your friend can then praise and pet the puppy, but must instantly stand up and turn away again if the dog jumps up.

This kind of training requires total consistency. Banish anyone from your home who says the terrible words, "I don't mind!"

left *Don't leave food where it can tempt your pet.*

Why is it a problem?

Stealing food from counter-tops and kitchen units is inconvenient and unhygienic; stealing from plates or hands while someone is eating is extremely bad manners!

Solution

Tidy up! If you leave food lying around, you cannot expect your puppy not to eat it. Prevent your puppy from begging for food at the table by never giving treats from your plate during meals or snacks. If your puppy approaches to beg for food, ignore him completely until he moves away and settles down, then praise quietly. Teaching your puppy to lie in his bed with a chew toy during meals works well.

digging

Why do puppies do this?

Digging is not only normal dog behavior, from the puppy's point of view it's fun, too! For some breeds, such as terriers, it's a pre-wired behavior that is almost impossible to

stealing food

Why do puppies do this?

Trying to cure "stealing" food is much like trying to "cure" eating behavior! Dogs are scavengers—indeed, their ability to eat whatever they find is at the root of their successful history.

stop completely. Wild dogs dig for many reasons—to find prey hidden underground, to scratch for roots to eat, to bury food, to create a shallow hole to sleep in, and for the protection of young puppies in the den.

Male dogs particularly may also scratch up the ground after they have defecated or urinated, to leave a visual marker that they have been there. Many pups dig for fun if they are bored and have the opportunity!

Why is it a problem?

For most owners, digging would not be a problem if the dog's excavations weren't right in the middle of the lawn! Digging also produces dirty feet, which then trample all over the carpets and furniture! Going to the door and shouting at your puppy may increase his desire to dig—he may perceive that you are barking encouragement, or be thrilled that he has got your attention!

Solution

For the vast majority of dogs who find digging pleasurable, it is usually best to attempt to redirect their behavior rather than trying to stop it altogether. Create a digging pit somewhere in the yard that is acceptable to you. Fill the hole with soil mixed with sharp sand, so that the drainage is good and your puppy won't become too muddy.

Take your puppy out into the yard and let him watch you dig in the hole and bury something really wonderful, such as a chew, biscuits, or toy. Allow your puppy to dig the object up and eat/play with it. Over the next few weeks and months, hide objects in the hole frequently. The idea is that if your puppy has his digging behavior rewarded in this area, he won't bother digging anywhere else.

left *Digging is fun! Redirecting this behavior is easier than curing it.*

above *All dogs need to let off steam, but an over-active animal needs to be calmed.*

Another alternative is to supervise your puppy in the yard and ensure he is constantly active and engaged in more appropriate behavior. Use interactive toys, such as a hollow "Kong" object stuffed with food, or an activity ball, to keep his mind off landscaping the garden.

crazy half-hours
Why do puppies do this?

Most puppies occasionally race around the home or yard, all four legs in a jumble underneath his body, as he uses the furniture and walls as agility equipment in a crazy "wall-of-death!" Such behavior seems to be simply a release of energy that snowballs into over-excitement.

Why is it a problem?

Although most pups soon grow out of this behavior, some may knock furniture flying or pounce on their owner at the end of the "race," biting and barking.

Solution

For some puppies, frequent bouts of manic behavior is linked to their diet.

If their diet is not suiting them, such behavior is likely to be seen about an hour after eating and they may be prolonged. (See page 86–89 to check whether your pup's diet is appropriate.)

Other puppies learn to persist with this behavior if their owners react in an exciting way. Laughter is often sufficient reward and any kind of shouting, grabbing, or squealing from children also exacerbates the situation. Calmly leading your puppy into another room, or leaving the room yourself for a few seconds, is usually enough to restore the peace.

coprophagia—eating feces
Why do puppies do this?

Many puppies eat their own or even other dog's feces. The reasons for this vary. Diet may be one factor, as may lack of confidence. Many dogs eat the feces of other animals, such as horse or cow dung—it seems to be a doggie delicacy!

Why is it a problem?

For the dog, it isn't! However, humans find this behavior most unpleasant, and certainly don't want to kiss their puppy afterward! Health and hygiene may be compromised through this behavior.

Solution

Check to ensure that your puppy's diet suits him (page 86–87). Try a change if you are suspicious that this may be an influence.

below Puppies often chew to relieve discomfort when their secondary teeth are growing.

Make sure that you wait with your puppy while he goes to the toilet and then immediately clear up the feces. Be calm and quiet about this. Some pups may resort to this behavior if they are inadvertently rewarded by your agitation. Teaching your puppy a really reliable "off" or "leave" command also helps (see page 118).

chewing

Why do puppies do this?

All dogs need to chew. Puppies particularly need to ease the discomfort of inflamed gums around teething time, and may also have a secondary "teething" period at six to

right All dogs need to chew—but it need not be something inappropriate.

eight months when the adult teeth establish themselves firmly into the jaw bone. Chewing may also release "feel-good" chemicals into the brain, meaning that some dogs may chew to reassure themselves when left alone.

Why is it a problem?

Dogs do not know the difference between a stick and a table leg, or an old slipper and a brand-new pair of sneakers. The phrase, "It's all chew toys to them" is exactly appropriate.

Solution

Give your dog plenty of safe chew toys! Toys that reward the dog for chewing them are ideal. "Kong" toys stuffed with food are designed so that small pieces of food are released while the dog is chewing, making the experience even more rewarding.

If your dog is chewing and ingesting inappropriate items, check that his diet suits him (see page 87). A small proportion of puppies chew to relieve boredom, frustration, or distress when left alone. Make sure you leave him for short but frequent amounts of time.

below *Redirect your puppy's attention to one of the many forms of safe chew toy.*

Before you go, give a rewarding toy to chew and play with that he does not have at other times.

nervousness
Why do puppies show this?
Nervousness is a coping strategy usually due to lack of experience. In a fear-inducing situation, a puppy who has not learned how to cope in any other way will crouch down, ears flattened to his head, tail tucked underneath his body. He may slink away and hide.

Why is it a problem?
If such anxiety is not addressed, nervousness may lead the pup to use aggression as a defensive strategy as well. Ideally, all puppies should be outgoing and confident in new situations, then they will be less inclined to run away, fight, or bite.

Solution
Substantial amounts of socialization and habituation are immediately required. Seek help from an experienced trainer or behavior counselor in order to set realistic goals for your puppy.

Beware of inadvertently reinforcing or rewarding unwanted anxious behavior. It may be tempting to reassure a fearful puppy, but this is easily misinterpreted as praise and reward for the fear itself. Ignore fearful behavior if possible, while praising and rewarding confidence.

aggression
Why do puppies show this?
Aggression is designed to increase distance between the dog displaying the aggression and the perceived threat. It is relatively rare for puppies to show true aggression, although play-biting and mouthing is often interpreted as such by owners. True aggression in puppies is nearly always based on fear. The puppy may fear the approach of another animal, person, or the loss of a resource, such as food or a toy.

below *Nervousness is accidentally rewarded when people offer reassurance.*

above Aggression between dogs can be difficult to resolve. Seek professional help if you are concerned.

Why is it a problem?

Aggression in any puppy should be treated seriously and treated with care, caution, and understanding to prevent it becoming a lifelong pattern. It is far more common for an owner to be bitten by their own dog than for a stranger to be attacked. The message is clear—seek help early!

Solution

Ask your veterinarian for a referral to a behavior specialist or rehabilitation trainer as soon as possible. Even if your fears about your puppy's actions turn out to be unfounded, you will learn a great deal about canine behavior and improve your relationship with your dog for life.

right Canine communication signals are learned early in life.

puppy becomes dog

No matter the size, shape, and breed of your pup, one thing is for sure—it's destined to grow into an adult! While many dogs do not fully mature until they are three or four years of age, true puppyhood only lasts as long as puppy teeth. These are replaced with a full set of adult canine teeth at about five months, and at this point, the pup enters a phase known as the juvenile period—or adolescence!

This adolescent period can offer a whole set of new challenges as your dog exhibits new behavior, and it is no surprise that the majority of dogs that fill rescue centers are between eight and 18 months old. "Teenage" dogs

can be difficult, belligerent, and downright disobedient! Despite months of work and effort put into good socialization and training, there are likely to be times when you wonder if you ever taught your puppy anything at all! Don't despair.

hormone problems

Much like human teenagers, dogs go through a period of social development where they test their boundaries, seem to be clumsy and uncoordinated, and can even appear to be "moody" for no reason. Much of this can be attributed to the changes that hormones make.

In males, the rise in testosterone—the male hormone—can make them want to be sexually active, challenge other males, and be selectively "deaf" in the

left This adolescent Collie is eager for a sexual encounter.

park, ignoring their owner's calls if they are exploring a particularly interesting smell! They also start to cock their legs when urinating and may even scent-mark with urine indoors.

Bitches can suffer from a canine equivalent of pre-menstrual tension before their season, and can seem irritable, particularly with other dogs. They may urinate more often before a season and lick themselves frequently.

For most pet owners these problems are easily dealt with by neutering. This reduces the frustration experienced by male dogs and the difficulties of keeping other dogs away from females in season, as well as the associated mess. Females can have their seasons suppressed through chemical intervention, although this is not a long-term solution.

However, even if you do have your dog neutered, it is unrealistic to expect that he or she will coast through adolescence with no problems at all.

above The young adult dog may not always be so co-operative as it was when a puppy.

keeping control

Many owners find that adolescence is the time when dogs learn how to pull on the leash, run away in the park, and generally test the boundaries of their independence. It is up to you to maintain training, socialization, and activities with your dog that keep him or her occupied and stimulated.

Go back to basics if you need to and retrain certain exercises if necessary. Join a class or group to give you support, as well as building on your previous skills with new activities, such as obstacle course training or teaching tricks. By now you will have the advantage of knowing your dog well, and understanding his or her needs. Building on this is not only rewarding, it is also ideal for cementing a lifelong partnership.

further training

Most puppies are a delight and grow up to be loved and valued members of the family. Occasionally, however, puppies cause problems that are unexpected, difficult to deal with, or even dangerous.

Most basic training problems can be solved, if not prevented, at a good obedience class. All dogs need training—it should be regarded as essential as vaccinations and good ongoing health care. Finding a good training class can be difficult, and a

badly run class can cause more problems than it solves. Follow the points below to find the class that's right for you and your puppy.

● Take personal recommendation from a trusted friend if possible.

● Make sure the instructor belongs to a professional organization that has assessed their skills, such as the Association of Pet Dog Trainers.

● *Always* go along to watch the class without your puppy before you enroll. The puppies and people should look relaxed and happy.

● Punitive methods or equipment should not be in use. Choke/check chains, tight slip collars, and prong

collars are not necessary and are totally inappropriate for puppies.

● Noise should be kept to a minimum—shouting is not necessary and lots of barking can indicate that the dogs are stressed.

● Instructors should be approachable. Do they appear friendly and caring in the best interests of owner and pup?

● How many puppies are there in the class? Every puppy should get some individual attention.

● Methods should suit the dog and handler in question. Food and toys are excellent motivators—few dogs work for praise alone.

below *A well-run, professional obedience class can solve problems and fine-tune your pet's training.*

● How old are the puppies? The upper limit should be 18–20 weeks at the start of the course, before pups lose their deciduous teeth.

● An hour's free play session may be fun to watch but could cause lifelong problems. Play should be carefully supervised and controlled and combined with gentle, effective training.

Persistent house training problems, possessiveness over food or toys, extreme fear of strangers or being outside, or any kind of aggression problem may require treatment from an experienced and sympathetic pet behavior counselor.

Most pet behavior specialists work only on veterinary referral, because puppies may suffer from clinical problems that cause behavioral symptoms, or may have had poor or bad experiences during early rearing that require some form of medical intervention or pharmaceutical support.

If you suspect that your puppy's behavior is not normal for his or her age, breed or type, seek help without delay. Ask your veterinarian to give your puppy a thorough checkup and refer you to a reputable behavior specialist or trainer who will be able to help you prevent the development of

above *A pet behavior counselor can help you solve serious problems.*

the problem and build for the future. It is also sensible to talk to your puppy's breeder, if possible. Most breeders have a wealth of knowledge and understanding about their favored type of dog, and although some can view their stock through rose-colored spectacles, the majority are often able to put new owners on the right track, ensuring that their puppy grows to become an ambassador for the breed.

index